Unbosoming

A Disclosure of Thoughts and Secrets

Cathy Vescio-Dibella

First published by Ultimate World Publishing 2022
Copyright © 2022 Cathy Vescio-Dibella

ISBN

Paperback - 978-1-922714-33-6
Ebook - 978-1-922714-34-3

Cathy Vescio-Dibella has asserted her rights under the Copyright, Designs and Patents Act 1988 to be identified as the author of this work. The information in this book is based on the author's experiences and opinions. The publisher specifically disclaims responsibility for any adverse consequences which may result from use of the information contained herein. Permission to use information has been sought by the author. Any breaches will be rectified in further editions of the book.

All rights reserved. No part of this publication may be reproduced, stored in or introduced into a retrieval system, or transmitted in any form, or by any means (electronic, mechanical, photocopying, recording or otherwise) without the prior written permission of the author. Any person who does any unauthorised act in relation to this publication may be liable to criminal prosecution and civil claims for damages. Enquiries should be made through the publisher.

Cover design: Ultimate World Publishing
Layout and typesetting: Ultimate World Publishing
Editor: James Salmon

Ultimate World Publishing
Diamond Creek,
Victoria Australia 3089
www.writeabook.com.au

Testimonials

Cathy Vescio-Dibella's must read 'Unbosoming' delves into the untold stories within her own backyard and beyond. A true inspiration from all walks of life, businesswoman, mother, educator and author. A wealth of knowledge, laughs and take aways. An all round insightful and intriguing publication.
Miss Ware

A compelling book written by a Melbourne hairdresser who shares highly personal stories that are written with humility, humour, and candor, and some hard hitting truths.

I have no doubt that at least one story from this book, will resonate with you.
Melbourne Youth Worker
Anonymous

This book is dedicated to Riccstar.
My heavenly angel, you will always be my 'Firework'

Contents

Testimonials	iii
Introduction	1
CHAPTER 1: My Memories, My Thoughts	5
CHAPTER 2: Your Stories: Real Names	57
CHAPTER 3: Danger, Manipulation and Bad Attitudes	113
CHAPTER 4: Mental Health and Addiction	127
CHAPTER 5: Sexual Encounters, Interludes and Invitations	173
CHAPTER 6: Violence, Harassment and Abuse	207
CHAPTER 7: My Lockdown, My Thoughts	233
About the Author	259
Appreciation and Gratitude	261
Acknowledgements	265
Conclusion	269

Introduction

'Unbosoming' is a collection of just some of the stories that I have heard and experiences I've had throughout my life, and in particular during my time as the owner of 'Think Innovation Hair and Beauty'. These stories cover a variety of different topics that over time provided me with a better foundation from which to learn more about myself and the wider community. I hope you find this book both practical and informative and in moving forward make time to nurture yourself, whilst also finding time to help others.

CHAPTER 1 My Memories, My Thoughts

This is a chapter about my own life and perspectives and gives you an insight into my world. My belief system, mindset and goals varied depending on my circumstances, but my persistence and determination to get the job done and to work things out never wavered, and motivated me to find positive outcomes. As a result, I became more resilient and able to embrace change. After all, change is happening all the time!

'I am built from every mistake I have made and continue to learn every day.'

CHAPTER 2 YOUR STORIES: Real Names

The use of real names in these stories is reflective of the trust that we can gain when we are connecting with others. Learning about someone's personal life has helped me to educate myself about the diversity and individuality of the people who I cross paths with. Listening to your story in one way or another has impacted my life in the most profound way. Thank you for allowing me to share some of 'you' in the hope that others are inspired as much as I have been!

CHAPTER 3 YOUR STORIES: Danger, Manipulation and Bad Attitudes

At some point in our life, we all fu** up and make mistakes – it is normal. The challenges that we face will vary and so will the outcome of what happened. What I have heard or what I may think makes no difference to anyone because just like me, I have no doubt that at times you have also been directly or indirectly involved in a situation that affected you in some way, just like some of these stories.

People say a lot of things and whether it is poor behaviour, attitude or circumstances we find ourselves in, sometimes no amount of talking will get you out of the problems you behaved yourself into!

Introduction

CHAPTER 4 YOUR STORIES: Mental Health and Addiction

What I have gained and what I have learnt about mental health and addiction is something money cannot buy! I have witnessed 'courage' and 'vulnerability' from people of all ages. One thing I know for sure is that any one of us can be impacted by mental health and addiction as it does not discriminate.

Expect the unexpected and do not be afraid to seek out the available networks that can support you in your recovery. You are important!

CHAPTER 5 YOUR STORIES: Sexual Encounters, Interludes and Invitations

There is nothing off limits when it comes to what I have heard or what I have experienced. The stories of sexual encounters that have been disclosed to me are no doubt stories that may resonate with you. Right or wrong, whether you are personally involved or know of someone caught up in a sexual interlude, it is happening, has always happened and will always continue to happen.

CHAPTER 6 YOUR STORIES: Violence, Harassment and Abuse

It is not uncommon to know of survivors and victims who feel isolated and alone as a result of trauma related to violence, harassment and abuse. To those of you who reached out and shared your story with me, I felt your heartache and pain, more than you know. My hope is that you find 'your' inner strength to continue to let others hear your story. By reaching out for support, you can play a vital role in your recovery. You are more than worthy of feeling safe and being happy.

CHAPTER 7 My Thoughts, My Experiences: Melbourne Lockdown

In 2020-2021 so many things changed.

Having the opportunity to write down my thoughts and feelings allowed me to process what was happening in my community, my workplace, my home, my surroundings and most of all my mind. What I did discover more than ever before was that I felt as though I was losing 'myself' in more ways than one! At times I felt empty!

Message to self: If I really want to live fully and wholeheartedly I must learn to slow down for long enough to remember, I need to reprioritise and reset so that I can realign myself with who and what I need most!

CHAPTER 1

My Memories, My Thoughts

A LITTLE OF 'ME'

Three decades have passed and over 35 years of hairdressing life. What an extraordinary journey it has been!

I would have never imagined that in October 1988, as a young, 18-year-old, just-qualified hairdresser, with not much salon experience, I would take over a business of which I was an employee. It was sudden and not at all planned.

What is more enlightening is that after 33 years I still run the same business, '*Think Innovation Hair and Beauty*'.

Developing and maintaining relationships with so many diverse individuals has truly inspired me to be open-minded to humans' unique differences, and my ongoing learning on both a personal and professional level has been interesting to say the least.

Unbosoming

Unexpectedly, in 2020, COVID-19; a worldwide pandemic occurred and everything changed! Residing in Melbourne, Australia and like so many others being at the forefront of extended restrictions in 2020, I was forced to take some time out from my work. This led me to find stillness and space. It led me to this very moment. A home retreat gave me the freedom to work on a personal project that has been on my mind for quite some time. I decided to tuck myself away to focus on me and my writing.

Throughout my time at the salon I have had the privilege of listening to stories and interacting with real people from all walks of life. This book is a collection of what I have heard and learnt and kept in my mind.

Being located close to the beach and blessed to be at a sanctuary that I love, amongst mother nature, has enabled me to be focused and to write. I feel blessed.

My mission is to share a plethora of secrets, confessions and conversations about life that many people have had with me. I have had to explore my memory bank as my mind was exploding and overloaded with content. Over the last 33 years, I documented so much in my journals and on scrap bits of paper which have enabled me to go back in time and allow these stories to flow.

I also wanted to incorporate a recollection of my own thoughts and feelings, collaboratively with these stories, so that everything you read is raw and real!

So why am I sharing what I remember in my writing?

I see this as a moment in time, my moment to release what I have heard, what I have seen, what stories I have been told. Many have opened up to me and we have had deep and meaningful conversations. There have also been toxic and negative conversations.

Overall, I have become more open-minded, my views broader and clearer.

At times I have also felt disheartened and completely empty while I have also had many moments in which I have felt a sense of vulnerability and sadness. My curiosity has led me to discover the unknown. I have continued to learn each day.

Moments have come and gone; they have passed by so quickly. What I have discovered as part of this learning journey is of utmost importance.

At times whilst you are reading you may think or feel that a story is about you or perhaps someone you know, but rest assured no names will come to light unless I have asked for your permission.

What happens within the walls, or at times outside of the walls, stays bound to me and to you. Albeit, if I trusted you enough and needed to chat, it is fair to say I also relied on someone to listen. If at any time I needed support or advice in relation to any information disclosed to me, I again assure you that confidentiality was always maintained. I have learnt so much as an individual and my purpose is to share these stories in developing an awareness, an understanding of others. By doing this we can better understand others' perspectives, lives and tribulations, in hope to live more harmoniously and to learn more about ourselves.

In advance, apologies to you if you find some of what you read to be offensive, cruel, downright awful and even fu**ed up. After all it is an expression, the voice of many, many different people, including myself!

These stories and experiences have shaped me to be the person I am today. My gratitude is with those who have shared and entrusted me with some of their journey. My hope is that after reading these stories you are positively impacted either in your thoughts or in your actions. I believe that when we listen, be kinder and love more, we can make a difference to ourselves and others.

> "The future depends on what we do in the present."
> **Mahatma Gandhi, Indian civil rights leader,
> 1869-1948**

A NEW DAY

When communicating and connecting with others, try to meet each other halfway and make time to listen. Allow your real presence to be genuinely felt and give people the attention they deserve. You may think your story is important, and it is, but so is someone else's story. We all have a story to tell.

With each new day, may you continue to explore and embrace the unique individual that you are! Do not be afraid to reach out for help or guidance when you may be feeling a little lost and confused. There are support networks available.

Be patient with yourself and others. Focus on your overall health and wellbeing with positivity.

Enjoy doing things that make you happy and find extra time to do them more!

A TIME TO LISTEN

After more than three decades of experience within a salon without a psychology degree, I have realised that hair stylists are some of the oldest and youngest psychologists helping people deal with the issues that they face on a day-to-day basis.

Hairdressers and beauty workers should be acknowledged for 'acting like makeshift counsellors'. I am 100 percent certain that a degree in psychology could have never prepared me for all the conversations I have had in the salon and what I have learnt. I am not just a hairdresser or stylist but someone who makes time to listen to stories. From the early days as a hairdresser, I became a good listener. I believe I became a therapist, counsellor, problem solver, friend, confidante, sister, mother, carer and so much more.

I vouch that other hairdressers would totally agree!

I support family violence education for our industry and believe there has never been a better time to bring these important topics of conversation to the forefront of our education system. Let us help one another so that we can better understand how to support those in need.

I encourage you all to book a training session via HaiR-3Rs website: www.hair3rs.org.au

Unbosoming

"Time is of the essence, but what is the essence of time?"
Karan Varsheni

BRING YOUR FOCUS BACK TO YOU

I look around me
I see motion
I think I am stationary
Yet I am moving too
The nature of this world is forever changing
I see all sorts of things happening to me, to others
Everything has moved in a different direction
It continues swaying back and forth
I just want to be still, in silence
What just happened?
In that moment, I see darkness
Yet I have learnt enough to see the light
I get in touch with that one thing, it is me
My oasis
My inner-soul
It is shining again
It is brighter
I smile

(September 1990)

CHANGE

Being confronted on many occasions with both personal and professional challenges has allowed me to have a clearer understanding of how life is continually changing and evolving.

The year 2020 has been a true testament to how change is ongoing and unexpected. In one way or another this change has impacted on each and every one of us.

As change continues each day, I want to focus on the positives outweighing the negatives in whatever situation I am dealing with. I know that in the long run it will be a lot more beneficial to my state of mind and how I would rather feel.

Moving forward I am excited for what each new day has to offer and understand that when we least expect it, change can happen!

All our emotions are relevant, open yourself up and nurture 'you'. Be kind to yourself.

Take the time to make improvements to your overall wellbeing.

COLOUR IN MY WORLD

Whenever I had a sleepover at Nonna's house I always made time to watch my Aunty Angelina put on her makeup. I became in awe of her creativity. Her mastery of colour always inspired me and as a young girl I learnt so much from her. Aunty Angelina's natural beauty, style and dress sense also set a precedent for how I've viewed fashion. I am so lucky to have such an amazing woman in my life who I've always looked up to.

Unbosoming

My aunty who lives in Germany may be a million miles away, but she will always hold a special place in my heart. Love you X

Another discovery of colour with a difference took place on a hot summer's day in Rye with my bestie Leesa. We were casually enjoying time out at the beach, gliding along the water in a little boat and just letting time pass us by. We were relaxing, laughing and chatting, excited to get a glowing tan. Unfortunately, it turned out to be more than what we bargained for! What we learnt that day was how important it is to slip, slop and slap that sunscreen on. As a result of not drinking water, not applying sunscreen and not wearing a hat, we both ended up with sunstroke and sunburn. Worst fu**ing feeling ever!
I am so happy that after travelling in different directions with our personal journeys in life, in time we found a common ground and rekindled our friendship. The best part is that we get to laugh about so many of our past experiences. Cheers to better times ahead.
Love you Leesa X

Much love to my Aunty Miriam who has always filled my life with colour. Maintaining a youthful presence at the age of 70 is something to be admired. You are a glam nan Aunty Miriam and we all love being in your presence.
I feel so lucky that we have maintained a special relationship and will always be grateful for the many life lessons I learnt and the secrets we shared.
The love we have for one another has never changed and best of all, my Aunty Miriam has never lost her natural ability to make us all laugh! Love you X

Colourful Samantha I am truly inspired by your courage, strength and attitude, in all that you do. The way you bring love and laughter into my life, our lives, certainly doesn't go unnoticed. With everything

you have experienced in the past and all that you are experiencing in the present in your own personal life you always make time to reach out to others. Such an enduring soul sister.
Rest up and recover my dear friend, we have a lot of great times ahead to look forward to. What a woman, Sassy Samantha!
Love you dearly X

> "If you want to go fast, go alone.
> If you want to go far, go together."
> **African proverb**

DID YOU EVER DREAM A DREAM?

Just over three years ago I was blessed to have met Ricc.
We fit so much into such a short time
For me and in you
the moments
the memories
the marriage of a friendship grew.

Ricc was so easy to love,
we were all drawn to his beautiful persona,
the way he lived life,
the laughter,
the smiles,
the real embrace of his hugs and kisses.

My husband Frank and our beautiful children Brooke and Corey
all fell in love with Ricc too!
Together our family friendship was gratifying for us all.
Riccy the RICCSTAR

Unbosoming

Magical Hands Hairdresser
Your time with us at the salon was without a doubt
Uplifting, energetic, fun
Your TEAM loved you! We all did!
And together with your TEAM you
Renovated
Redesigned
Rejuvenated the salon and of course we had to have the eggplant colour back wall.
You insisted! And you made it happen!
You certainly left your mark on the walls in more ways than one
An everlasting impression.

You were a Rocking Red Hot Pimp at our 20-year celebration
You loved every minute of it and we had an awesome night!
You sure did know how to party it up! 'Scooby' King!

Our clients
Your clients
All of us
Everyone wanted a piece of you
It could've been
A hug
A kiss
One of your beautiful gestures
The way you would open the door for people
That sparkling smile
Those magical hands
You were in demand baby
Simply by just being Riccy!

My Memories, My Thoughts

On a personal note
Ricc and I just connected instantly
Our friendship was made effective immediately...thanks to cousin Anna.
Ricc has been like the dream friend
The one you would always want to have in your life
"Thank you" Ricc would say...I would say "no ...Thank you!"

My life has been enriched; our lives have been enriched
I am so humbled
I am so grateful
I have learnt a lot by his wisdom
His knowledge
His love
On February 2nd 2010 Riccy's life path had taken a different direction
Together family and friends were there for him
Ongoing, each and everyday
A visit at home or in hospital
A phone call, a text message
A meal, a 'scoob' or two or three
And best of all the communication...the conversations, there were many!
Ricc you were never alone, and you were always so dignified.

Scotty I am so grateful to you for being you!
Nurse Scotty when you said you were in it for the long haul
You meant it!
Together you were each other's universe
and together you were there in those final moments
the way Riccy wanted it to be.
Ricc is now resting in peace
He has flown with the birds into his paradise

Unbosoming

and Ricc when you told me
that in your next life
you wanted to come back as a white swan
well, the white swan you shall be
Beautiful
White and Pure
Soft and Fluffy
Calm and Serene
Gliding casually along the waters
With the sun shining on your back

You are to us all
A lifetime of Love
Beautiful Memories
Magical moments
Awesome fun times
You left a big and beautiful impression on us all
You touched our lives
Ricc you will live on in my heart, our hearts forever

We love you

(7th February 2011)

My Memories, My Thoughts

FAITH, RELIGION AND SOCIETY

What I do know is that
I feel like we are living in a crumbling society
Religion tends to separate people
Equality really does not exist
World peace just is not a real thing
And never will be
I also believe that
It is up to us as individuals to maintain our own happiness
To find peace within ourselves and around us
When it comes to religion follow your own faith
Do not have expectations that others will support your beliefs
It is your journey
It is your personal choice to believe in what you want to believe!

FEAR

I have learnt that fear is natural and sometimes helpful and when I embrace change it can open my mind to other possibilities.

I make sure that I spend time in wanting to understand more so that I can fear less!

FEELING FAB AT 50!

On Saturday 1st February 2020, all day, the rain persisted, and Mother Nature delivered waters from above, making her presence known. At times the rain came down strong and heavy. I sat still and watched it purifying the earth with not one ounce of concern about my 50th birthday party that was planned for the day.

I was blessed to have my family and friends help with setting up and everything just seemed to fall into place. Everyone knew I wanted this gathering to be fuss free. It was a day that needed to flow, with patience and positivity. And it did!

It was late afternoon and progressively my nearest and dearest began to arrive. I was elated and bursting with anticipation for the intimate group of people who would share in this special milestone with me.

As an addition, I decided to book in a surprise for my guests. I was excited to have 'The Calmer Miles', a gorgeous couple Dee and Kev entertain us with their chilled vibes and catchy tunes. Having their presence was so fitting to the ambience I wanted to create, and I am so happy they were a part of my celebration.

At around 8pm that evening the rain had decided it was enough and it just stopped! There was a moment when I got lost in my thoughts and found myself gazing up at the sky in between the pop-up gazebos.

To my delight, graceful and very still, dusty pink heavens from above appeared. At that very moment I knew that the rain was a blessing from angel Riccstar. The brightness of the sky began to engulf me, and I knew that Ricc's presence was embracing me.

I am extremely grateful to all the lovely souls who made my day so very special. It was my kind of party and I had an amazing time! Bonus, the enjoyment and freedom to smoke 'scoobs' went down a treat!

Turning 50 never bothered me at all. I remain 21 at heart!!

FESTIVE SEASON, OR IS IT?

Christmas time is different for everyone. Our experiences, our family dynamics and our past can influence how a Christmas Day plays out. When I hear my clients venting and saying, "I fu**ing hate Christmas time sitting around with my fu**ed up family, it pisses me right off", I am not surprised as I have heard words similar to these on many occasions. It seems to be an ongoing conversation that happens around festive season and you would be surprised how many people vent about this very topic over and over, year after year. For many, it's not so festive after all!!

Just like many family situations that may not always be perfect, harmonious or conform to the norm, my family is no different.

How we value family is also completely individualised depending on what circumstances you may have been faced with as part of your life journey growing up.

But then I ask, what is a normal family supposed to look like? How is a normal family meant to act?

I definitely don't think I, nor anyone, can answer that. What I am sure of is that all family dynamics will be different and that is completely okay!

Despite family politics, I fu**ing love Christmas and the festive season.

GIFT OF GIVING

Whenever I knew that Barlow or Delilah were coming into the salon for an appointment, I was so excited. I wanted to make an addition to my personal storyline because I valued this family and how they conducted themselves.

Barlow was the CEO of a multi-million dollar company, married to Delilah and together they had two beautiful daughters, Quinnie and Magenta.

Delilah reminded me of a bohemian goddess. Her style of clothing, long chocolate brown hair and overall presence was stunning. Delilah taught yoga and had the loveliest personality to compliment her natural beauty.

Barlow was always very charismatic, polite and had you drawn into his conversation from the moment he started talking. One thing I loved about him was how he always took an interest in others. He would want to know something new about me or my family and would say, "Enlighten me with what's happening in your life Cath. How are your family doing? Have you been keeping well?"

Barlow would also remember everything about our previous conversations and took a genuine interest in my extended family who he had never met. He always told me how lucky I was to have grandparents. "Cherish them," he would always say.

I can honestly say that whenever Barlow came into the salon for a haircut, I was all ears, just listening and intrigued by him.

Delilah was also a person who would ask about me and how I was feeling and although she had never met my parents, her asking about them and how they were doing was so appreciated.

I fell in love with this family. They were all truly graceful humans, and I always felt a sense of calmness when I was in their presence.

It is so wonderful when you meet people who constantly gift money to charity organisations and show support to those who are less fortunate. This is exactly the type of special people that Barlow and Delilah were and I was so blessed to have crossed paths with them.

I will always be grateful to Barlow and Delilah for the many influential and positive conversations we shared and for teaching me, as a young businesswoman at the age of 18, that having lots of money means fu** all.

In true Barlow words, "Sharing is caring, right?"

Barlow and Delilah, Quinnie and Magenta,
YOU ARE ALL HEART; PURE, GENEROUS and AUTHENTIC.

(A humble family who did not want to disclose their real names).

GRATITUDE

I have come to realise that it is only when you take a leap off the ledge of familiarity that you really start to find out who you truly are, and most come alive.

You don't have to chase extraordinary moments to find happiness as quite often it is right in front of you and can be found by paying attention and practising gratitude. I never underestimate the power of community, connections and conversations as these have been such an influential part of my journey to date. I will be forever grateful to the salon, my second home. Every person who has ever come into the salon has in some way contributed to my personal and professional learning.

Get up each day and allow yourself to be a little more curious about new adventures, new experiences and new beginnings. Who knows what tomorrow will bring, but today venture on, keep going, do the best that you can for 'YOU'.

HAPPINESS

All of us will experience positive emotions and life satisfactions that can generally make us happy. When we connect and get involved with like-minded people who make us feel good about ourselves it contributes to experiencing more positive than negative feelings.

Being successful isn't the key to happiness.
Happiness could in fact be the key to success.

Do not wait until life isn't hard anymore before you decide to be happy.

Unbosoming

HUMAN CONNECTION

As a young girl growing up I was always quite inquisitive and in tune with what was happening around me.

The power of observation was and still is a huge part of my personal learning.

Take a moment and ask yourself...

Are you present and engaged when others are talking to you?
Are you really listening?
Are you genuinely taking the time to ask how others are feeling?
There is a lot more to a person than what you just see on the surface.
Unfortunately, I have often seen some of the most important things go unnoticed!
I encourage you to look a little deeper.
Reach out to others.
We all need human connection and human interaction.
Ditch the technology for a while.
Make time for face-to-face communication.
This is when the most special connections and friendships are made.

> "One kind word can warm three winter months."
> **Japanese proverb**

INDOLA LEGENDS

Anyone who has been lucky enough to experience an 'Indola Legends' conference would agree, we have all been extremely spoilt. Year in, year out, for almost 20 years, together as a team we have travelled all over the world. I can honestly say that the conferences I attended have been the most amazing, extravagant and fu**ing best times ever!!!

The laughs, adventures, activities and the wild and crazy moments that we experienced, will never be forgotten. I have the best memories to cherish and have maintained some beautiful friendships thanks to Indola and 'Saska Group'.

Thank you to all the creative hairdressers and business owners that I was lucky enough to meet. The support I received and the many conversations we have shared have been a platform for my ongoing learning. Overall, you have in some way contributed to helping me to develop into a confident, and resilient businesswoman. I am so happy we crossed paths and hope that in the near future we have a big reunion and get to party like the good old days.

Cheryl, Gabby, Helen, Lynnie, Marki, Marie, Mel, Sharon and Teresa, amongst many others, I love the catch up sessions that we still have even after so many years. Whether our gatherings are online or in real life, makes no difference. We always have the most wonderful time and I just think all you woman are fu**ing legends!

Love you all X

INNER PEACE

I have always been a person who is concerned about how other people are feeling.
I want to be sure that everyone is safe, feeling good and not in any danger.

Unbosoming

I am a lover not a fighter.
To see people hurting each other does not sit well with me.
I want to save the world and make the environment we live in a more harmonious and an enjoyable society.
Realistically, saving the world is not possible.
I do not think world peace will ever happen.
What is possible is that if we surround ourselves with like-minded people who have the right intentions to see each other happy, then this is the path we should be taking.
If you are at peace with who you are, then it will make such a big difference to your day to day living and people will notice this about you.

There is a feeling of peace,
There is a feeling of tranquillity.
There is a feeling of serenity,
There is a feeling of love.
And there is joy.
The power of these fundamental feelings are what we crave,
Don't fight it.
Conquer these feelings,
Let them find you.
Let yourself find those feelings,
Embrace them.
Then there will be you,
Absorbed in peace.

(10th July 1994)

IN THE KITCHEN

How powerful is the kitchen table!

It is the place to sit around with family and friends and allow time for communication to flow and connections to be made. It is a place for asking questions, sharing in some banter and laughing. It can be rewarding on many levels.

One of my favourite things to do is to gather with people and cook for them, especially at my home.

When sitting around you can always find something to talk about.

I always tend to choose a wine based on images or words that intrigue or catch my eye. Most recently in true 'me' style, my purchase was influenced by the label, ironically titled 'Small Talk'.

If you are ever visiting an Aldi store, do yourself a favour and look out for 'Small Talk' Shiraz. Read the label on the bottle and then proceed to buy it for only $5.99.

Take it home and make yourself merry with a glass of red. Get some 'Small Talk' happening and refer to the questions on the bottle as a starting point...and then keep going with your own set of questions!

Enjoy time with your loved ones, whether it be family, friends or work colleagues and engage in some interesting conversations. Salute!

Just in case it is not available any longer here is an example of the conversation starters 'Small Talk' Shiraz has to offer:

Unbosoming

What do you wish you had placed in a time capsule 15 years ago?
If you obey all the rules, do you miss all the fun?
What's your ideal superpower?
What's your favourite number? Why?
Passenger or driver?
If you had to change your name, what would your new name be?
What word or saying from the past do you think should make a comeback?
What is your guilty pleasure?
What song always puts you in a good mood?
What's worse: Laundry or dishes?
Where would you like to travel to next?
What seven-letter word is spelled the same way forwards as backwards?
What is wrong but sounds right?
What is the most refreshing thing on a hot summer day?
What random stranger has had the biggest impact on your life?

Preparing and cooking food with others can be the beginning of a great conversation, a casual chit chat or just some 'small talk.'

Appreciate the time together, the food and then bon appetite, take pleasure in the cuisine, whatever it may be!

My Memories, My Thoughts

LIFE LESSON (one of many)

Over the summer break after completing Year 10 in December 1985, I got a Saturday morning job at a salon in the Moonee Ponds market. This place was a real funky, hip salon and I loved it. I would get up extra early on Saturday mornings and get the V-Line country train to work. I was excited and committed to my little part-time job.

If you've never experienced a country train ride, do yourself a favour and organise to have a day out! Ask any of my friends and they will tell you that to this very day I still love train rides!

I turned 16 in January 1986 and kept my first salon job until I finally found a full-time apprenticeship. I only completed one term of Year 11 and was so excited to be leaving school to pursue my dream.

My hairdressing career was now a reality and for about three months I travelled extensively. I would commute daily as a 16-year-old on the country train from Craigieburn to Spencer Street Station and then commute on a suburban train out to Northcote. My mum would pick me up on Thursday nights when I had to work late and that was a big deal back in the day. With two young children and a long road trip from home, it was a big commitment from her to do this week in week out. I will always love my mum and am so grateful to her for all the running around she did for me and my older brother Lozza.

I immediately loved the salon environment and was enjoying my workplace. I felt like a real grown up getting my pay each week and enjoyed treating myself to vintage clothes from the op shops on High Street near my workplace. Walking the streets each day, travelling solo and finding my independence was without a doubt one of the most rewarding and grounding experiences as a young girl. I became streetwise as a result of these teenage years.

My employer was a male, ten years my senior, and his sister also worked at the salon. Not long into my apprenticeship, I found myself making an unexpected decision when I was faced with an uninvited touch and feel scenario. The behaviour from my boss caught me off guard. I knew then as a 16-year-old that I made the right decision to never go back into that salon.

There was a day when only my boss and I were working. I was in the back room practising how to perm on a mannequin head when from behind me, he proceeded to put his hands over mine touching my fingers and the perm rods whilst also pushing his hard groin and body quite firmly up against me. It was not invited and as a young girl, I felt vulnerable and afraid. In that very moment, I knew that it didn't feel right for this man to be touching me that way.

I had always been a bit of a tomboy growing up and knew not to take shit from anyone. As his embrace became firmer, I had a sudden urge come over me. I shrugged him back quite aggressively and in a loud tone so that my voice could be heard, I told him to get the fu** away from me and to fu** off!

I proceeded to get my belongings and stormed out of the salon. I went to the public phone box and called my mum, telling her to come and pick me up and that I hated my job.

I never told anyone what had occurred that day and it was only a few years ago when I shared this story with my mum and some family members. I also recently told her how one of my male family relatives tried to open mouth kiss me when he was really drunk. It was the sloppiest most disgusting thing ever! I was 14 years old, and this incident was also uninvited!

Now in my early 50s the advice I would give to my teenage self would be to use the word "fu** off" a little more frequently because some people just need to be told!

The outcome from my job did not deter me from following my dream to become a qualified hairdresser. In fact, I became mentally stronger and more aware of people around me. With eyes wide open, I felt empowered to move forward, pursuing my passion.

With the support of my parents, I went to the Australian Academy of Hairdressing where I would continue to embrace what I was so interested in pursuing. It was a breeze being there and I truly loved learning everything to do with hair and beauty.

About two months before I graduated, my time at the Academy nearly didn't come to fruition! I got caught up in stealing products with some of the other students and we got busted big time!

My mum was informed and since my parents were paying the tuition fees I was exempt from being expelled. This was in contrast to my fellow students who were a little older and paying their own fees – they were very unlucky and didn't get to complete the course and obtain their Cert 3 qualification in hairdressing!

During my time at hairdressing school I was blessed to have formed a special friendship with Anna. Each day we had lunch together. I ate apples and healthy foods, and Anna would always eat chips and pizza. We laugh about this all the time!

Despite the fact that Anna was never allowed to come over to my home because her parents were extremely strict, we have maintained our relationship for more than 35 years and are still best of friends. Each time we get together we always talk about the good old days and our laughter and banter always gives us belly laughs. Love you Annie X

LOVE OF LIFE

Often, we question our existence.
Who am I?
What am I doing?
How can I be a better person?
What is my life's purpose?
What kind of love serves me?
Are we supposed to fall in love with just the one person?
How do you define love?
What is real love?
How can you love more?
What do you enjoy doing that you love so much?
What can you do to show more love, more compassion towards others?

My love of life is about living in the moment, and I am driven by the search for meaning in everything I do.
I am a deeply spiritual person who thrives in an environment seeking a higher sense of being and would like to continue exploring this about myself.
I enjoy stimulating spaces and do best when I am challenged, mentally and spiritually.
I see life as an adventure.

Connecting face to face and conversing with others on the big philosophical questions of life is what I enjoy.
Whether I am spending time in a vintage market, walking along the beach, listening to music or meditating in a quiet garden, I am nourished when I am helping and serving others.
In my career at Think Innovation Hair and Beauty my journey has been nothing short of exactly that! It has never been just about the haircut!

MAGICAL DREAM

Flying wings of an angel,
You made it happen,
I know you did.
Where is this journey taking me?
How do I get off this ride?
Which path am I taking?
Where will the crossroad start?
Where will it end?
Do I follow my instincts?
Travel in time,
In the moment,
In the now.
This situation is like no other.
It is delicate!

Angel wings sparkle around me.
I have casually taken a step.
One step at a time,
I made my way to you.
I sat with you.

Unbosoming

Your angel wings were soft and warm,
I loved being in your embrace.
You smiled when you saw my tattooed arm,
It has purple and green stars for you.
Lady bugs for me, for us.
We spoke about so many different things.
We loved hard,
We got 'Scooby' high.
We laughed hysterically,
Our feelings and emotions were pure and real.

I told you how amazing you are,
In the heavens above.
Everyone is missing you,
My family just adore you.
We are forever loving you.
I don't want to leave.
Quietly you whispered in my ear,
You told me to turn around.
Take one step at a time,
Walk down the path.

You told me I had things to do,
To get on with life.
Places to visit,
People to love.
You look at me,
I look back at you.
I know you are with me in spirit always,
You are special.
The love is solid, as it always has been and always will be.

(April 2016)

At times our subconscious mind is revealed in our nightly dreams. This was one to remember and one that brought warmth to my heart and soul.

MINOR ACCIDENTS

Reflecting on my younger years, I must have been very accident prone, or just in the wrong place at the wrong time.

I broke my nose when I was five after being chased by my older brother, Lozza, and my nickname growing up became squash nose!!

I totally understand how it feels to be living with a negative complex about yourself! I was always getting picked on and got bullied about my squash nose. It is not a nice feeling! I had to wait until I was a fully developed young woman, at the age of 16, to have a 'nose job'! Thank fu** for that!!

I also got hit in the face by my brother when I was the wicket-keeper, and he was batting! He swung and went to hit the ball, spun around and I copped it again!

And how can I ever forget the day I was hanging out with my friends in the cow paddocks at the end of my street. I was rolling around in a big aluminium cylinder, laughing with everyone rolling faster and faster, getting dizzier and dizzier and then oops….an accident! I ended up slicing my right hand and had to go to the doctors to get stitches. To date the scar is still visibly clear and will always be a reminder of that day!

Another time I was riding my bike freely while daydreaming, not a worry in the world, when I went head first into the neighbour's parked truck. As a result, a massive lump surfaced on my forehead! Ouch!

On a holiday in Lakes Entrance, I was up on the top bunk when a bug ended up dropping into my ear and decided to take a crawl through my ear canal. Growing up and to date, I have always had a good pain tolerance but fu**, that bug pain was the worst! Every time that sucker crawled, the pain kicked in like nothing I had ever experienced before.

The trip to the hospital seemed like forever and lying down on my mum's knee was the only comfort I had. I knew Mum would make sure everything was going to be okay. Luckily as soon as we got to the emergency department of the hospital, they attended to me straight away. With the suction of a mini vacuum type device, that little sucker came out, alive!!!

Another near accident was when we were away in Eden and my intoxicated uncle decided he would give me a driving lesson. In a flash I accelerated so quickly and in the next moment I pushed so hard on the brake that we both nearly ended up through the windscreen and over the tent set up in front of us. Crazy times!!

Getting picked on about my nose for so many years put my fighting spirit into overdrive and I learnt how to defend myself. I do not put up with shit from anyone and can still vouch that I am that person today! I have a voice and when I need to I can roar!

My Memories, My Thoughts

MY THOUGHTS ON...A to Z

Attitude – Determines everything
Bubble baths – Make more time for them
Career – If I am doing what I love, it never feels like work to me
Dream – To live in Byron Bay
Equality – Fight for fair
Fun – Laughter, socialising and entertaining people
Gin – I enjoy it however it is served
Happiness – Making others happy
Independence – Helps to shape the person you become
Judgement – Go with your gut instinct
Kindness – Important for us all
Ladybugs – Special to me
Music – Soulful
Night out – Start with a Fireball shot
Optimism – Makes you happier
People – Interesting
Quality – Over quantity
Resilience – Continue to work on yourself
'Scoobs' – Enjoy and don't abuse
Train – My favourite lift on an outing
Understanding – Listen and make time for others
Volunteering – Willingly find time to get involved
Wisdom – Keep learning
Xena – Hospitable, friendly and welcoming
Youthfulness – To remain young at heart
Zeal – Energy or enthusiasm in pursuit of a cause or an objective

Perfectly sums up my thoughts overall!

Unbosoming

NEW BEGINNINGS

An important life lesson is learning to respect that people are who they are.
We may not always agree on the same things, and that's ok.
We also don't have to stay connected and that's ok.

Do you need to accept the behaviour of someone when it just doesn't feel right?
Why do people think we need to stay connected with others if we're not comfortable around them anymore?
Who you want in your life and who you don't is up to you.
Your decisions shouldn't be influenced by others.

Have a voice, have your say.
If there is an opportunity for a reconciliation, well great – move forward and re-build that relationship.
If you decide to go your separate ways, ensure that you take everything that's happened on board, learn from it and look ahead to your new beginnings.

Your world is big and wide, with varied fields of hope.
Do not let the words of another, let your dreams fade away.
Allow the warm sensations you feel to brighten your own day.
Think about the excitement of what a new beginning could look like.
Find courage within yourself to keep moving forward.
Anything is achievable, if you believe in yourself.

My Memories, My Thoughts

NO THROUGH ROAD

Craigieburn was a very small community in 1988 but it was still much bigger than when my family first came in 1975. In my teenage and young adult days I always referred to Craigieburn as paddocks and cows, because clearly that's what my family home was surrounded by. We lived at the end of Alma Street, and it was a no through road. At the end of my street, it came to a stop – you couldn't go any further. It was all fenced off and this is where the cows lived, lots of them. As kids we would muck around and have heaps of fun in the paddocks that also led you to the local milk bar, hot bread kitchen, and one of the fish and chip shops in Bank Street. I travelled this route often and would meet friends along the way. We would order our fish and chips and just sit and talk in the park across the road. We would take our time and one by one, chip by chip we savoured in every moment. The best was ripping the paper off the top of the wrapped-up bundle and relishing in the warmth of those hot chips. If I was lucky enough to have some extra money, I would treat myself to a potato cake. Yum!

To all the families who lived in Alma Street back in the day, thank you for the memories and fun times! We certainly did have the pleasure to enjoy the freedom of country living.

Growing up in the 70s and 80s was priceless!
I felt as free as a bird!

Unbosoming

PERSONAL GROWTH

Life is not always what it seems.
We will have ups and downs, highs and lows.
There will be good, bad and ugly moments at different times and for different reasons.
There will be happy times, there will be sad times.
Our experiences and challenges in life surprise and confront us, unexpectedly.
Whatever happens can be big or small, difficult or quite simple.
Nevertheless, life is made up of these moments and there will be many of them.

Imagine the challenge of:
- A baby learning to crawl
- A prep student learning to read
- An eight-year-old running wanting to win a race
- A teenage girl experiencing her menstrual cycle for the first time
- A teenage male's voice changing
- The experience, excitement and nervousness of that very first kiss
- Sitting for a driver learner permit
- Getting your driver's license
- The nervousness you may feel going for that first job interview
- A student completing high school and making decisions about where to next
- Experimenting with drugs and alcohol
- Understanding death, the loss of a loved one
- Enrolling into university
- Starting an apprenticeship or full-time job
- Experiencing sex for the first time
- The excitement and feeling of falling in love

- Getting married
- Becoming a parent
- A grandparent, and on and on it goes.........

There are a million different experiences and challenges I could go on about, but the reality is that each of the experiences we encounter throughout our lifetime are our own and they belong to us.

How we deal with challenges will vary depending on age, circumstances, influences and decisions.

Ultimately 'YOU' get to decide and in some unexpected ways you don't.

POWER OF OUR EMOTIONS

It is normal to feel down, overwhelmed or sometimes sad about different situations.
Feeling angry, powerless, worried, stressed, anxious or unhappy is also very normal.
Unfortunately, these feelings can get out of control, and can take over people's lives when situations are too intense.
It can be scary when people are angry as it means they may act irrationally or unlike themselves and serious problems can occur.

Reactions to emotions are your responsibility.
They are our reactions to situations, things, circumstances or people.
Do not leap to reactions without taking a minute to think about it.
Try to figure out the reaction and what it should be.
Allow a moment to stop and react in a way that is safe and respectful rather than acting out of emotional chaos and creating problems.
Be mindful of your wellbeing and safety and look for positive outcomes.

SAND

Life and living is certainly a journey like no other.
I believe that when we connect or disconnect from people in our lives we learn, grow and develop into our own individual selves.
Relationships with family, friends, acquaintances, work colleagues and our pets are bonds that are forever changing.
It is these bonds, these connections that help us to understand not only ourselves but others.

When I sit on the beach and pick up a handful of sand, I let it flow and fall through my fingers until there is only just one grain left.
I know that if I keep repeating this over and over, I will never find that exact grain of sand again.
That one grain is unique just like 'you' are unique in your own way.

We live in a society where comparing ourselves to others is becoming common practice, especially amongst young teenagers.
Self-identity is being compromised and tarnished by the need to keep up with someone else.
Our phones, iPads and laptops can overload us and at times become toxic especially when it comes to social media.

If we want fewer distractions, we need to be more mindful of the amount of technology we use. We need to take a break from it all and allow ourselves more real-time, face to face connections with people.

When we learn to embrace our unique self and come to understand that we are very special in our own way, just like that one grain of sand, anything is possible.

My Memories, My Thoughts

SEEN BUT NOT HEARD

Growing up during my teenage years, I always enjoyed being around older people. I would absorb the communication as a learning tool and grew to understand more about the diversity of different individuals. Whether it was family, friends or just hanging out in the community, I most definitely enjoyed listening to others who were chatting in my presence. I would listen to who was saying what and why. I would always ask questions as though I was an adult myself and was often made inclusive in conversations.

My parents come from a European background; both having been born in Italy. They have always been modern and have a down-to-earth attitude. I think Laurie, Luci, Michelle and myself didn't give them much of a choice. We made our parents open-minded to the modernised Australian way of life and living, and encouraged them to move with the times. Over time, they allowed us the freedom to be who we wanted to be, even if they weren't always happy with our choices.

The family home we grew up in was loving, fun and very busy. It was also a disruptive and chaotic environment from which you wanted to escape at times! Overall, our space was a platform for any type of communication, and everyone spoke openly about many topics.

My mum would often vent her concerns to me, and I absorbed a lot of that information and stored it away. Those conversations provided me with a stronger mindset, and I am grateful to her for that!

We would always have a house full of relatives and friends and we didn't shy away from much. I would hear the terminology, 'children should be seen and not heard' and that 'kids shouldn't interfere and disrupt adults when they are talking'.

In our family home, as I got older, I learnt to utilise my voice. If I wasn't comfortable with what was happening around me, I began to speak up and often this got me into lots of trouble. I never backed down. Today I continue to stand up for human rights, for fairness, equality and safety for all.

My personal life has had no shortage of highs and lows and I continue to face many of my challenges head on! The experiences I have had have allowed me to learn more about myself and become a more confident individual.

I truly believe that many of the real life situations that I faced growing up played a major role in helping to shape the person I am today. The connections that I have made over the years with mature-aged people from my early childhood have taught me an abundance of knowledge. I have gained so much from these conversations.

If I was being fair and truly honest with myself, I'd say that tapping into people has always been a real thing for me. I want to know who you are. What's your story? What are you thinking? What can I learn from you? Can I help you with anything?

I want to continue to nourish my mental state of mind, for me, and for those around me.

SELF ESTEEM AND INSECURITIES

We are all unique individuals, and it goes without saying that it is so important for everyone to work on positive strategies to help ourselves feel good. Too often we get so consumed and upset by the opinions that others may have about us. The fact is, there will always be people in our world who we like or dislike and that is okay.

Self-esteem is a state of mind. It is the way you feel about yourself and is noticed by the way you behave and act. It is your 'internal belief system' and the way you see yourself in the sense of your worth as a person. Low self-esteem means poor confidence and that causes negative thoughts which means you are likely to give up and not try rather than to face challenges. High self-esteem will help you to be a more confident and happier person who is motivated with the right attitude to succeed.

Self-esteem is made up of the feelings you have and positive thoughts of yourself.

The number one barrier to success is the inability to believe in yourself. We often tend to overlook our strengths and focus on our limitations and negative talk. A 'self-belief system' encourages an optimistic and constructive way of thinking and acting. This in turn leads to positive results at home, school, in the workplace and within the wider community.

We all have something that we may not like about ourselves and believe me it is quite normal to feel this way. My 'squash nose' nickname made me feel like shit! I did not decide on the nickname I got, but I endured being bullied for years. Although I can laugh about it now, as a vulnerable young person, it did not make me feel good about myself.

In our lives there are many different reasons why we feel insecure. How we deal with our thoughts and feelings can be very challenging. Each day people are facing personal insecurities. Many of these setbacks include self-doubt, jealousy of others, self-image, weight issues, feeling overwhelmed about upcoming tasks or challenges, and becoming annoyed by the behaviour of others, amongst many other issues.

Believing in 'YOU' and embracing your self-worth is important.

It may take time, but 'YOU' are worth it!

> That thing that makes you "Not fit in",
> Be proud of it. Nurture it.
> Because that's your
> Extra in the ordinary.
> **Myra S.**

SELF REFLECTION

I have learnt to accept that some things in my life will never be the same. I am comfortable in knowing what I know and am embracing the change!

They say people come into your life for a reason, a season or a lifetime. This is so true!

Sometimes what we think may have been a forever relationship for some reason changes and it isn't what you may have always thought it to be.

I know that in time people may heal, reconnect and rebuild relationships but there are some you just don't want to revisit. Doors closed!

As I mature, this is becoming more apparent to me. I understand what works for me, who I need or want in my life. I have also come to realise that letting go of the past is beneficial to my moving forward!

What I continue to learn is that if we focus on the importance of staying connected, maintaining healthy relationships and reaching out to others for support, together we can make a difference in each other's lives.

It is just as important to let go of what does not really fill your heart with joy anymore and take it on board as one of your life experiences. Let it go to move forward.

Our attitude reflects the choices we have made.
We all have the freedom to choose.
We can respond positively or negatively.
It is not the event, but how we respond to that event that ultimately determines our attitude.

SETBACK

Business can be so rewarding, particularly when you know you are the person who has provided employees with opportunities not only to be employed but to learn skills, and grow and develop as a person. There have been ones that may have left to build their own business however the biggest personal setback has been when they have left to set up their own hairdressing business literally around the corner.

Regardless of what others may think, in the world of hairdressing, this ongoing scenario still happens, and it can profoundly impact a business in many ways!

Despite a variety of different views and opinions on this touchy subject, I know exactly how it feels to be in this situation. I have had to rebuild my salon business and grow my customer base over and over. It takes time and effort, and a lot of energy!

It would show much integrity if an employee who leaves a salon to venture out on their own builds their business in a new suburb, with a new clientele, and let the clients that love them so much, follow. They will find you.

I employ staff and invest in them wholeheartedly, so yes I am entitled to feel let down when this happens!

I am not a machine; I have feelings too!

SMILE

When you become extremely unhappy or have feelings of sadness,
Don't be so hard on yourself.
It is okay to be overwhelmed.
Emotional rollercoasters can take control of us, unexpectedly.
We have all experienced a time in our life that saddens us.
Sometimes you feel as though nothing else matters.
You are at a low point, you feel alone,
You just want solitude.
Be patient.
It takes time to get back into life, into reality.
Remember that happiness can spring within you.
Allow yourself time to bounce back,
You can do it.
You can and will smile again.

You will be pleasantly surprised,
And it can happen when you least expect it.
The darkness begins to fade away.
The power of happiness and gratitude resurfaces.
You start to bloom.
The light has been turned on.
You did it!
It has always been within you,
Embrace the glow.

(March 1990)

"The most wasted of all days is the one without laughter."
Nicolas Chamfort – French writer, 1741-1794

STREETLIGHTS

Growing up back in our teens we had a curfew. Be home before the streetlights come on or not long after! It felt safe and I had some of the best times as a teenager growing up in the 80s. My teenage years contributed to helping me become more street wise and aware of my surroundings.

The best memories I have had growing up in my neighbourhood was getting to know those who lived around me, my neighbours. The after school gatherings; playing cricket on the street, 'kick to kick' footy, hide and seek, roller skating, 'elastics', hopscotch and many other activities requiring us to connect. The excitement of coming home each day after school played out in my mind even before coming home. It was not only a time of fun but also a time of learning about each other's cultures, ways of life and families.

Many of these experiences taught me the importance of accepting others' differences.

It is sad that these days we live so close to our neighbours yet are so distant. So many people say that they do not even know who lives next door.

I dream that when walking the streets I see more children 'hanging out', making connections and enjoying their neighbourhood. It is a shame that young kids and teenagers spend time indoors and not outdoors amongst others!

My hope is that we go back in time to embrace those experiences that enrich us as people and that those street lights keep shining on.

THANKFUL TO THE 80% and a little thankful to 20%

The past 33 years in the salon has come with no shortage of challenges. As a businesswoman today I am thankful to past and present employees who have supported the salon vision. In return I have been happy to allow my employees the freedom to be independent people who have been able to make the salon space their own. Many have helped me to create what has been achieved and I would not be where I am today without this.

I want to express that I have been extremely lucky to have had 80% of those employed to be great stylists and wonderful people whom I have loved being around. You know who you are, and I love that we are still in contact. Maintaining a mutual respect has not changed. It is those foundations that have genuinely formed great friendships.

And then there have been 20% of those who have been employed who were not quite the hair crew that I needed, for different reasons! Whether you fu**ed me over or hacked my social media page that went viral immediately, you taught me more than you will ever know. So, thank you!

It was with immense thought that a decision was made to sell my business in December of 2019. It was a decision that was not made easily but it was time for me to move on. Who would have known that after three months of making this decision, a Covid-19 disaster would begin?

Moving forward I would like to transition out of the salon and my hope is that an excited, energetic and passionate person is ready to walk in and take over an established and successful business. Think Innovation Hair and Beauty has the potential to keep growing and flourishing!

For me and for now, there is only one direction to move in, and that is to keep going until a new owner takes over.

WHO SAID WHAT?

Salons are places filled with an abundance of conversations. Often, I cannot keep up with who is talking about who.
What I have heard, learnt and understood within my salon walls have held me in good stead.
The theory of listening twice and talking once seems to make a lot of sense.
So many conversations that I have had confirm that as humans, all people do speak about one another. At times in a positive manner, at other times in a negative manner.

Unbosoming

I am sure we all know people that fly under the radar. They are the ones who on the surface seem to be one type of a person but underlying are someone different.
These people do really well at getting what they need out of others and can often be unnoticed.
If anyone ever says you are two-faced, don't take it too personally.
It's reality that people talk about people!
If anyone ever says they don't talk about others, I call it bullshit!

We all know that chit chat amongst people happens and if I had to line up 100 individuals in front of me right now and ask the question, "Have you ever spoken about another person in a negative way?" I am pretty confident that everyone who is honest would respond with a yes.

One thing I am certain about and have learnt over time is that people can dismiss you very quickly if you don't serve a purpose to them anymore.
If you don't agree with their views, suddenly they view you differently!

I encourage you to speak your truth, have a voice and stand up for what you believe in.
Be your authentic self.

> "In order for you to insult me,
> I would have to value your opinion."
> **Anonymous**

My Memories, My Thoughts

WORK-LIFE BALANCE

Take the time to ask yourself:

What do you seek in life?
How will you nurture yourself?
What are three things that you really enjoy doing that make you smile?

What I have come to realise since the beginning of the pandemic is that trying to maintain a work-life balance is crucial to our mental health and wellbeing. As important as it is to consume our time in our workplace, it is as important to consume our time looking after ourselves. Being part of Melbourne lockdowns has given me the opportunity to focus on a variety of hobbies that were always pushed to the side, due to being consumed by my work. For me it has been as simple as being outdoors in my garden, creating a peaceful sanctuary, with minimal resources. I have been so grateful to 'bric a brac' from family and friends. It is also a reminder that 'someone's trash can be someone else's treasure'. My garden has truly come to be a space filled with many treasures.
As difficult as it has been to keep motivated, I have come to realise that keeping an active body and mind is essential. So, go out to seek, explore, be curious, make a plan, set some goals, pursue a hobby and always find time for yourself.

Staying true to yourself and finding happiness will impact your life in the most wonderful ways.

Unbosoming

YOU ARE ALIVE

My resistance to reality fades
I am placed in the most precarious of situations
Reality sets in
But then I open my eyes
I take another step forward
It is a new step
It is a brand new day
I stand still
Very still
Peace will find me
Or I will find peace
Allow your inner beauty to find you
That person is inside of you
You exist
It is within us all
Be present as you hold still
Live that moment
As you breathe, it is obvious
Your existence is obvious
You have been given life so this could happen
Don't underestimate it
Your existence is very special
There is one happiness by nature
You are alive
That is happiness
We look
We search for it
Did I forget that peace is searching for you?
The road is straight
The road is now winding and bending

The road is built to give you access
To go up and down, around and around
The magic in this life is to really understand
Understand what?
Why peace is looking for me
I need it
You need it
We all need it
I search for it
And all the while I do not understand

(March 2017)

YOUR INNER BEING

In life, pay attention to not only your physical and emotional health but most importantly your internal self-belief system. Be more self-aware. Our wellbeing, state of mind and our self-worth is imperative to being a happier human.

Change can happen if you are prepared to bend a little.
Seek help when you need it, make time to talk to someone.

If you are an angry person, work on strategies to find calmness.
If you are unkind, nasty and unpleasant to be around, ask yourself, "How can I change this behaviour?"
The very essence of who you are and who you want to become lies in your hands.

We all experience these emotions at some point in our life. As humans, it is normal. What needs to sometimes change is the reaction we have to some emotions. It is our responsibility to be more aware of ourselves and change for the better.

CHAPTER 2

Your Stories: Real Names

ANGEL STACEY

I am so blessed to have crossed paths with Stacey and her beautiful family.

I will never forget the day of Princess Stacey's farewell, the horse and carriage and the words that Donna shared with me when we hugged.
"Go home and hold your daughter and tell her how much you love her."

To this very day I feel so privileged being able to spend salon time with Stacey's mum Donna, who is a gentle soul and such a sweet woman. Bonus for me was getting to know Stacey's nan Diane, who is also such a lovely person.

Unbosoming

During her illness, I could not imagine the thoughts and emotions Stacey was experiencing. On the day of her funeral, Stacey's insightful and profound message was shared.

YOUNG HEART by Stacey

"If I can say anything the journey so far has taught me to live each day, not plan too far ahead as you never know when something can change. Change doesn't have to be scary, it's just an adjustment. I can't stress enough to you all to not hold back in life. Live it, breathe it, be it. Smile for you're alive, give a friendly hello to someone, tell people that you think they're great. Small things can change someone's day for the better."

In Honour of Stacey Jayne Taylor
(10th February 1992 ~ 22nd January 2016)

BAHA

"Music is the last true voice of the human spirit. It can go beyond language, beyond age, and beyond colour straight to the mind and heart of all people."
Ben Harper

I read this quote more than 15 years ago at 'Baha' in Rye and yes, it was definitely the No. 1 Live Music Venue on the Peninsula.

I instantly fell in love with this place and the people who ran the venue, Nathan, Nick and Jahna. They were all genuinely beautiful souls and I always felt at ease and comfortable at the Baha.

Shout out to Nathan who always made time for my boy Corey. No doubt he will visit you one day on his travels.

In 2010 I celebrated my 40th birthday at the original Baha, a little intimate venue that was truly my go to place each year, summer or winter. I will never forget that special night for so many different reasons, especially knowing 'Ricc was there in spirit with me'.

As the venue's popularity grew bigger, a new premises just up the road came to life. I can honestly say there was never a shortage of chilled vibes, a heavy dose of original live music from the nation's greatest artists and to top it off, they served up beautiful, fresh Mexican cuisine. In both locations, I along with many others have had the best memories to cherish.

Baha had a 70s feel to it and the ambience was always relaxed and engaging. I loved meeting with the locals and communicating with people I had just met. I found the space at the Baha to be exciting and liberating and could not get enough of this hip little venue. Everyone was down to earth especially mid-year when all the holiday makers weren't around.

No matter when we popped in for a night out, we were always welcomed with a big smile by the amazing team.

Smoking 'scoobs' was a thing, table tennis challenges were fun, and the winter fire pit was a bonus! To top it off, listening to the talented artists and dancing the night away was my kind of treat!

Baha always had a community feel to it and provided a space and stage for any up-and-coming artists to showcase their talents. The 'open mic' night was made available to anyone who wanted to sing a song and yes, I even got up a few times and sang my little heart out!

Baha transcended into the most awesome platform for anyone to share their music.

What a bonus it was to be at the Baha one evening with my daughter Brooke to see 'Tones and I' perform live! Totally amazing!

Baha became a place where opportunities would come to light and for many, dreams really did come true! I miss the BAHA!

BILLY

"My son is on drugs, it's killing me and our family, what can I do? What if he ends up dead, what can I do to help him?"

This conversation is ongoing. I have heard so many people cry out for help.

Over the years it is becoming more apparent that way too many people, particularly the young, are experimenting with drugs. I am talking as young as eight and nine years of age. So many families have been confronted with these types of issues and many parents and families just don't know what to do.

Any family or person can be affected, even those who least expect it!

Over the last three decades I have met lots of young kids. Whether I got to know them from my children's friendship circles, the salon or within the community, I can honestly say they are good kids and have been respectful towards me. These young teens are beautiful souls. Many come from loving families and some from dysfunctional circumstances.

I have personally seen many of them grow up into young adults and have gotten to know a little more about them through conversations that we have had. One thing for sure is that over that time I have witnessed how successful, talented, loving and skilled these kids are and still continue to be.

The connections made with family and friends also gave me more insight into their private lives. I have seen firsthand that there can be a turning point for the better. Unfortunately, most of the time, before you can see positive outcomes, it is very common that family members, friends or even strangers associated with someone who is experiencing any of these issues, will ultimately be affected either physically, mentally or emotionally.

It is normal to feel as though you just don't know what else you can do to see your loved ones get better. I have seen parents try so hard to seek out help, support and advice and at times they just have felt lost and helpless!

Despite how you have been raised, your upbringing doesn't discriminate when it comes to addiction. Some of the choices young teens make are not always in their best interest, but nevertheless they make those choices anyway! Just like Billy!

I want to share some of Billy's story in the hope that others think about the consequences of taking a drug, commonly known as 'ice'.

Billy came into my family home at the age of five. It was my son's birthday and entertaining a houseful of energetic boys and girls was great. I miss watching all the kids playing together, laughing and having a ball. I wish I could go back in time and relive those days when our kids were young and innocent.

Move forward ten years and a whole new chapter begins.
Did I ever imagine that Billy would fall into a trap of drug addiction? Absolutely not! The things I see and remember when I think of Billy are positive attributes that I love. He was such a talented footballer and always has been. Billy is kind, has a gorgeous smile and this reflects what I have always felt about him. When Billy puts his mind to it, he is a great worker with good work ethics. Deep down Billy can be vulnerable, as we all are at times, although I do believe that with patience and time, Billy will begin to feel more confident about the special young man that he is.

The choices Billy has made often led him to a pathway of desperation and self-isolation. When heavily influenced on ice, things got ugly and out of hand.

Being addicted to drugs and going into survival mode is where an element of danger sets in. Billy's mental state of mind has been influenced and controlled by ice; the drug substance he was consuming way too often. Whether you have smoked and inhaled drugs, injected or swallowed them, without warning you begin to lose sight of your inhibitions. Suddenly a different version of you comes to life and takes over your whole being.
When Billy was on the run from authorities, we would arrange the appropriate time that he could visit the salon, so that I could cut his hair. Each time, he flew under the radar. I never had any hesitation in making these moments happen. In fact, I wanted to see Billy and would always speak to him the same way I would if he was my own son.

Over a five-year period, Billy had two jail experiences. There are some very interesting scenarios that occurred behind bars. Unfortunately, I am not able to disclose any of that information. I can say that I learnt a lot from the conversations that Billy and I shared. Our chats were an open discussion for anything to be spoken about. Although at the time my messages weren't being absorbed, I kept trying. I cared about Billy and worried each time he left the salon. I still see the little kid in Billy, the one with the big cheeky smile and a heart of gold.

To this very day I am still connected to Billy's family. For years I have, in a roundabout way, been on this journey via the many conversations that I have had with both his parents, Scotty and Mandy. I have repeatedly witnessed the fear, frustration, despair and worry. I have watched the anger that has been felt, the tears that have been shed, and the silence when as a parent, you just don't know what to say anymore.

There were so many times I witnessed Scotty and Mandy feel helpless and lost. Jake, Billy's brother, was also mentally and emotionally scarred by what was happening to his little brother. Everyone felt distraught and defeated. All they really wanted to do was to help Billy and make him better. It was so sad to see them all going through this nightmare!

Watching one of your children suffering from the implications of ice addiction rips all the goodness out of you and makes you feel numb. Your inner world crumbles and you become desperate for answers. At times, many times, there are no answers. Everything is at a standstill.

Time goes by and there is a continual uncertainty about whether the person will pull though. Is there a turning point for the better?

Unbosoming

The problems continue to escalate and manifest into so much more; more than I ever had imagined. The end road for some can momentarily be jail or in the worst-case scenario, death.

Billy is aware that there are no right or wrong answers in how he can best approach the setbacks he was faced with. He fu**ed up repeatedly and understands that he is accountable for the choices he has made. Reminding Billy of all the great qualities he has is a key step in his recovery. Believing in himself and wanting to rebuild nurturing and positive relationships can play a major role in the outcomes that lie ahead. I hope Billy opens his mind up to self-love and embraces who he is. Billy's journey ahead will certainly come with many challenges, but what he has learnt holds a lot of substance and depth. With ongoing support from family and friends, my hope is that Billy can find positive ways to help himself work though the issues that he may be facing.

I have hope that new beginnings are possible after being an ice addict. When least expected, you start to reconnect with the person you once knew, and you begin to see yourself smile again. Billy can reinvent himself and become a better version of who he once was.

There is so much discussion to be had around the topic of drugs and any other type of substance abuse. It is very important to understand that relapsing is a frequent and natural occurrence for many during recovery, and any addiction comes with no shortage of challenges.

My hope is that anyone experiencing any type of addiction finds it within themselves to be their own source of strength and inspiration. You are important and special, and the teacher is you. You play the biggest and most important part in your recovery. Anything is possible, if you believe in yourself.

To all of you who have let your guard down and shown me a vulnerable side of yourself, you are extremely brave. As an individual and as a parent myself, I have learnt so much. You have shared very personal and in-depth information that has allowed me to understand more about your concerns and what you were dealing with. In turn, it sparked a passion in me to continue wanting to help others, especially young people.

I look forward to watching a new and improved version of Billy. My hope is that he believes that he is worthy of a better life, and that the road once travelled reaches a turning point for a clearer and safer journey ahead.

CARLOOCH

When I first met Carl I thought he was the most gorgeous teenager with the mind of an old man. I immediately fell in love with his aura. I remember telling my daughter Brooke when Carl left that evening that I hoped she would continue to stay friends with him and that they should grow old together. That was in the year of 2010, and now in 2021, we are all still connected. Carl will always be family to me.

Carl is a quiet, mature, respectful, intelligent and gentle soul with a heart of gold. I just love being in his presence. Carl and I formed our own little friendship and I always tell him that he is the other child in my life. We often spend time together alone. Whether it is a market trip, a beach house retreat or a beach walk, I can honestly say it is always special and I just adore Carl so much.

Christmas holiday time in Rosebud became extra special with an added addition to our family when Carl began to join us year in and year out. I amongst others wanted to adopt him. All my family friends wanted his attention, his presence and on many occasions, they were blessed to have got to know him too.

Carl always makes a genuine effort to communicate with people. His calm and natural beauty is worth every moment when you are in his space and to this day I am more than blessed to be able to spend time with him.
In the year of 2016, Carl's dad, Rob, was unwell and I witnessed Carl watching over him during this difficult time. I was so inspired by Carl and the way he handled the situation he was confronted with. At this time, I learnt so much more about Carl in the way he managed himself. Whilst his dad's health deteriorated, together with Carl, his mum Cath, and their extended family, I was regularly present to support them and be by their side.

I did not really know Carl's dad well, but I soon realised that much of what I knew about Carl was a reflection of his dad in more ways than one. Whenever I would pop in to visit Rob I was always greeted with a beautiful big smile. The conversations that followed were nothing short of informative, interesting and filled with real substance. Rob had so much knowledge about so many things. I would always look at him and wonder how he knew so much about so many topics. Rob would always tell me that he loved reading and listening to music and that if we all continue to read a little more that we would be able to keep learning. They say that reading is knowledge and Rob was certainly a reflection of this statement!

It was only after one visit that I discovered Rob had a sweet tooth. Each visit after that day I always greeted Rob with a cappuccino and a treat. When I watched Rob eating his sweets it was like watching a kid in a candy store. He smiled the whole time, and you could just see the enjoyment all over his face.

Aside from knowledge Rob was also very creative and artistic and was just so handsome to look at. As Rob's health deteriorated, so too did his memory. Rob started to refer to me as "you're here" rather than by my name. Despite everything, Rob's big, beautiful smile always welcomed me each time.

When Rob passed away I went to his farewell, which was so personal and intimate. The service was transcending, and all Rob's personal and special belongings were on view for us all to admire. I will always be grateful for the moments that I was able to spend with Rob and in return am extremely lucky to have Carl continue to be a big part of our family.

I knew from the first day I met Carl that he was gay and knew it would only be a matter of time before the conversation came to life. When Carl eventually told Brooke I was so happy! I couldn't wait for him to tell me! It was a market day outing and Carl and I went on a little road trip. We were chatting away and more than halfway to the market Carl still hadn't mentioned anything. I decided I would initiate the conversation and said, "Carl is there anything you want to tell me?" Well Carl just burst out laughing and said, "I am so glad you brought it up, I was waiting for you to say something to me".

What a day of liberation and freedom!!

We had the best chat and I told Carl how excited I was that he could finally be him, the real him! All I ever wanted was for Carl to have the freedom to love who he really is and most importantly to feel comfortable within himself, in his own skin.

Taking ownership of being your true authentic self and embracing 'YOU' is when you can really start living your best life.

I love you so much Carlooch X

DAYS AT THE OAKS

When I was in Grade 5 I met the most gorgeous little prep student who had milky white blonde hair and cute freckles on her face. Her name was Brooke. I instantly took little Brooke under my wing and mothered her like my own. I loved her and as the years passed by, I also grew to love her family. I knew that I would one day be a mother to a girl named Brooke, and sure enough that happened thanks to little Brooke T.

My first ever Ladies Oaks Day outing was with her mum Pam way back in 2001. I wasn't sure if it would be something I would enjoy, but yes, it was the most wonderful day out! I didn't ever drink bubbles until having the pleasure of being amongst these women and that day set a precedence for me enjoying bubbles too! I still go to Oaks Day each year and love the excitement of dressing up, wearing a hat or fascinator in my hair. I smuggle my flask into the racecourse and have a quick squig to top me up and we always enjoy smoking a 'scoob' or three before kicking on to our next venue where we party on late into the evening!

It is always a great day full of laughter and having a little flutter on the horses to add an extra element of fun. We meet and chat with people along the way and on many occasions, I have even made my way into private guest areas. I work my magic and before I know it, I am in the marquee eating and drinking for free, mingling and enjoying myself.

Your Stories: Real Names

Thanks to my friend Jobe, lucky for me, about seven years ago I was gifted with two yearly tickets to Oaks Day. I am forever grateful to have met this beautiful man who is achieving amazing outcomes within his local community and surrounding communities. I always got so much out of the chat sessions that Jobe and I shared and believed that he would flourish in whatever he chose to pursue in his career. I am so happy for Jobe and all his accomplishments to date, especially becoming a daddy to a beautiful daughter.

One of the best experiences on race day was in the private function area with a hairdressing company that I have been associated with for many years. In true form I managed to bring a few people into the private event and together we enjoyed, food, drinks, music and the company of my fabulous hairdressing colleagues, especially Dario.

At the end of the day a trip back into Southgate for an afterparty was organised and once again I worked my magic and had Angelo, Laura and Moreno join us on the bus ride into the city where they also got spoilt at the private party. It was free. It was amazing and they are memories I won't ever forget. Since the last Oaks Day that I spent with Angelo and Laura they became parents and were blessed with baby 'M' Micky. Miss you and love you all XXX.

I cannot finish this story without mentioning an ice cream treat with a difference! Imagine leaving the races on Oaks Day, well any race meet for that matter, and amongst the confusion of people, taxis, trains and limousines a Mr Whippy van is spotted. Ronnie walks across the road, has a quick chat, makes a deal, a cash exchange and before we knew it, Sandy, Dafney and I were in a self-serving ice-cream van on our way to our next party destination. Each year Mr Whippy would be waiting in anticipation for Ronnie to venture out of the track. He would hail Ronnie over quickly and off we would go on our merry way.

Yes, that is exactly what happened, and it was our way out of crowds for three years in a row.

From primary school beginnings, when our daughters met, to now, Ron and Sandy are one of the most beautiful couples I know.

Everyone needs a friend like Sandy!

Love you guys so much XX.

> "The only thing that will make you happy is being happy with who you are."
> **Goldie Hawn**

FOR THE LOVE OF VERONIKAH

It caught me by surprise when out of the blue one day, at the salon, I was confronted with some home truths from an employee, Veronikah. I was shocked with the information she had disclosed to me about herself.

"I have been stealing shampoo and conditioner from the salon for over 12 months now and I am so sorry. If it is okay with you I would like you to take the money out of my salary each week until it is all paid back. I really am sorry, and I hope you can forgive me."

Prior to what I was just told by Veronikah I already knew that her weekend benders were getting out of control. I was concerned about her, yet also respectful of the fact that whatever Veronikah did on her days off was completely her business.

In all honesty when re-opening the salon each week on a Tuesday, Veronikah was always ready to work. Her clients seemed relatively pleased with her services, her weekly salon revenue wasn't impacted and Veronikah had a clientele that continued to grow. She very rarely took sick days and overall, her commitment and input to her work showed a level of maturity and responsibility.

What I did know and had known for quite some time was that Veronikah was consuming party drugs week in, week out. Having lived in Craigieburn myself since the age of five, growing up here and working in the same community meant that I knew lots of people. It wasn't long before this information about Veronikah was being shared with me. What I was being told wasn't always pleasant but having known Veronikah since she was a young 16-year-old and loving everything about her, I just continued to let her personal journey belong to her!

As the months passed and I began to find out more and more about Veronikah, it was noticeably obvious that her body was becoming more withdrawn and fragile. Her weight loss became more evident, her face seemed tired, and her skin colour was more pale than usual. Unlike the Veronikah that I knew, things slowly began to change. She started to take sick days and would often look a little worse for wear.

The best part about this story is that Veronikah never changed in terms of her friendliness and kindness towards others. These beautiful qualities about her remained the same back then and to this very day!

Once Veronikah confessed about her lifestyle and antics, it became a turning point for her.

At that same time I now had the opportunity to discuss with her everything I knew about her weekend lifestyle outside of the salon. I remember telling Veronikah that if she didn't pull up and start taking better care of herself that I would no longer be able to employ her. I also made it very clear that some of the ongoing conversations and the reputation that she was instilling on herself were also having an impact on the reputation of the salon. Her connections were too close to our workplace and too many people knew too much, including me.

Things needed to change for the better. This is exactly what I wanted for Veronikah and her family.

It wasn't too long before Veronikah decided to go on a self-discovery journey of her own. At the age of 21, in October of 2013, Veronikah enrolled herself into a life skills program called 'Landmark'. She had asked if she would be able to have a Saturday morning off from work so that she could take part in this course. I never had any hesitation in allowing Veronikah to go and find herself via a new positive learning experience.

The program was delivered over a few months and as time went on I genuinely loved what Veronikah was telling me about 'Landmark'. Whilst Veronikah was exploring her way through the course, I could sense an energy and flair about her that was endearing and welcoming. It was something I had not seen from her in a while. I was more than happy that this was the beginning of a new and improved Veronikah and to this very day am blessed with her presence!

During the time that Veronikah was participating in 'Landmark' she came to me with an idea about a fundraiser. After some in depth brainstorming and discussion, 'Funky Forest Flair', a live Hairshow, was created and directed by Veronikah. As a salon team and with the support of family, friends and clients, this hair show came to life!

Funky Forest Flair was held at a boutique bar in Bourke Street, Melbourne and some of our clients, family and friends took part in the show modelling for the event whilst many others volunteered their time helping out.

Mandy Sharman was our photographer, and the music was on point with DJ Phuoc. Cara Drake supported the event by donating all the clothing from her fashion label 'Calouda' and is now in her own right a successful designer.

Collaboratively we raised in excess of just over $10,000. The money was gifted to a rehabilitation centre in Sunshine, Victoria, a refuge that provides crisis accommodation for women with children who are experiencing alcohol and drug issues. Overall, it was a real success and a true credit to Veronikah and everyone who got behind her to support such an important initiative.

Veronikah's life has become enhanced on so many levels because of her ability to make changes in her own life. These changes have all been for the better. Over time she has continued to make noticeable improvements, and these certainly haven't gone unnoticed. In 2016 she took on the responsibility of becoming the salon manager and performed remarkably in this new role.

Her managerial position lasted for three years and in the middle of 2019, Veronikah multi-tasked her salon commitments alongside the beginning of a university degree in Psychology. By the end of December of 2019 Veronikah decided to dedicate her time to study more and work in the salon less. I supported her wholeheartedly with her decision.

Fast forward to July of 2021.

The salon is definitely a platform for learning, and I am so happy that Veronikah is at university studying Psychology. The salon environment and the connections that Veronikah has made along with the many conversations that she has had will no doubt hold her in good stead when she begins this new and exciting chapter in her life.

Since January 2020 Veronikah has been working as a casual senior stylist. She is always in great demand and getting an appointment with Veronikah is a first in best dressed scenario.

During the past 12 years that Veronikah has been a part of my Innovations family she has enhanced my life immensely. In some ways Veronikah's reality became mine. I have learnt so much from her and still do to date. The roads we have travelled and the journeys we have been on together in and out of the salon is nothing short of precious to me.

P.S. You are so much more than you will ever know, and I am so very proud of you!

I love you Veronikah X

'HAI' ON LIFE

A friendship with Hai is everything you could ever imagine and more. He is a beautiful person. It is a special friendship of a rare kind. An absolute gem!

There was never any doubt in my mind about taking Hai under my wing.
When the opportunity arose, thanks to Tracey, I welcomed Hai with arms wide open.
What a genuine, caring, kind, selfless human being this man is!
Spanning more than two decades of getting to know one another, Hai remains true to himself and is one of the dearest people in my life.
Humble, honest, generous and so damn funny.
His silly antics make us laugh all the time.
His cuddles are warm, snug and feel so real.
And Hai has a pure heart with so much love to share.
Everyone observes that Hai has a 'happy go lucky' attitude and will often comment about how wonderful it is to see him laughing and joking all the time.

Hai is always ready to greet you with a smile; his aura beams with radiance and he has an energy about him that is uplifting and inviting. In his presence you always feel safe.

He loves my tummy, and it is a common occurrence that when getting a hug he will squeeze my 'squishy' as he calls it, and we just laugh.

Taking Hai on an outing is always an adventure.
He is curious, open-minded and will always take care of you.
Our Thursday evening nightcaps are always enjoyed and the catch up conversations we have are a bonus.

In true form, Hai keeps us on our toes with his stories, where often we are left wondering…

Above everything that I love about Hai, I know he is a kind and caring father full of love for his son.

Unbosoming

I have no doubt that Lennox is the heart and soul of Daddy Hai. When you get to travel again Hai, I hope a catch up with your son is on the agenda!
Hopefully soon!!!

You are dearly loved, Hai X

Your Stories: Real Names

IMPROVING BEHAVIOURS

Growing up I was raised with European parents and knew all too well how things operated in my own home, much of which I didn't agree with or like. I would stand up to my dad about everything that went against what I believed was not right. The outcome was not always pleasant.

I continue to educate my dad about his attitude and the way he treats my mum and am proud of the improvements he has made over time. I have learnt to enjoy the company of my dad more and have watched as his mannerisms and behaviours have changed for the better.

Dad has issues that he encountered in his childhood that in many ways are a reflection of him today. He never dealt with the challenges he faced growing up and although he may appear to be resilient on the surface, in other ways he is just as vulnerable as you and I.

Spending time with Dad has made me aware of his upbringing. Listening to the stories he shares has contributed to understanding more about him. My dad has many tales to tell. His survival mode when growing up wasn't always ethical, nor was it smooth sailing.

As far back as I can remember, when people meet my dad they think he looks mean and scary. He really isn't! When he raises his voice, he just seeks control. He is still coming to terms with learning how to communicate effectively at the age of 74! When Dad comes to realise his outbursts aren't warranted nor acceptable, and he calms the fu** down, we laugh and move on. There have been many occasions when Dad has apologised to me. This is a big step in his personal growth and a credit to him.

I believe I got my mischievous and rebellious traits from my dad. We are both strong-minded, don't shy away from speaking our truth and although most of the time he thinks he is in the driving seat when we go head-to-head in confrontations, rest assured I don't give up very easy. They say we need to agree to disagree, well not always!

Dad and I communicate openly about everything and I don't hesitate in asking questions that catch him off guard at times, even if it rocks the boat a little. I know deep down he is listening and is better at understanding what acceptable behaviour is and what it is not. He will often have a laugh when responding and still likes to have the old school mentality of the man being right, but I am always quick to reply, "No, sorry Dad, no go zone!"

Keep up with trying Dad, you are doing better, and I love you for that!

IN FULL BLOOM

When Jess and I first met, I instantly felt a positive connection towards her and was pretty confident that I wanted her to join our salon family. Luckily for me, Jess became one of our team members and I am so grateful that she did!

There was something very special about Jess. In a brief interview we had in the little front room of the salon I could sense that this young woman was determined, fierce and very self-assured. I was not wrong! In our conversation that day Jess shared something personal about a medical condition. At the age of 18 she was diagnosed with a kidney disease (IgA nephropathy). Despite everything I just got told, Jess assured me that she was good to go, and everything would work out just fine.

So, in August 2010 Jess was employed and that is when she began her journey at Innovations. During her time at the salon Jess earned herself a reputation of being a talented, friendly and engaging senior stylist who we were blessed to have on our team.
It was only six months into full-time work, in February 2011, that Jess started one type of dialysis (peritoneal). Trying to maintain a full-time job whilst also having to do dialysis at home was a challenge in itself.

Despite everything that Jess was trying to manage both personally and professionally, her endurance and ability to keep going was a true testament to just how courageous she really is.

Not quite three months had passed and by April 2011 Jess started to experience heart problems. This latest setback had Jess visiting the hospital three times a week to complete haemodialysis therapy. That is the time that Jess went on to begin part-time employment, as a way of being able to manage both her working commitments and focus on her health and wellbeing treatments.

At the age of just 20, Jess started going into complete kidney failure and heart failure. It was not long before complications commenced and Jess needed a donor due to the kidney failure. In July 2011 Jess was gifted with a kidney by her uncle Bruce Wilson.

A couple of days after the transplant Jess was given a drug that gave her a severe anaphylactic reaction and she nearly died. Jess ended up in ICU. Somehow I was determined to make my way into ICU so that I could see Jess, and although I was told I could not see her, I was not leaving until I did! I casually made my way into the area outside of ICU, waiting for the right moment for that door to open and for me to enter. I walked around looking in each bed until I found Jess.

When I looked at Jess, she seemed so fragile and pale. Her body was connected to all sorts of tubes and machinery, and it was alarming! I stood beside her, put her hand in mine and began talking to her.

I told her how much I loved her, kissed her forehead and smiled at her saying, "Jess you are too young to die. You are not going anywhere because you have a lot of life left in you and so much travelling to experience." There was so much more for Jess to accomplish, and I genuinely felt that everything was going to work out. It had to!

I did not stop talking to Jess. Although she was not coherent or responding, I knew that she could hear me!

And just like that, out of nowhere a nurse came up to me and asked who I was and how I got in. I replied with, "The door was open, and I am Cathy, Jess's aunty". The nurse looked at me a little puzzled. I smiled at her and said, "I am leaving now, Jess is going to make it, everything will be okay". And just like that I casually left ICU, the same way I casually entered!

For a few months after getting out of ICU and recovering well, Jess tried to maintain her working commitments as best she could whilst also recovering from all that she had been through. Then Jess had another setback. In October of 2011 she needed another surgery to clear a blockage. Thankfully the outcome was a successful one.

I believed that Jess was going to have a turning point in her life for the better after everything she had been through, and in time she did! I believe that what Jess went through made her reassess her life and herself. Her direction, her priorities and her focus shifted onto bigger and better things. Even though Jess left school at the age of 15 without even completing Year 10, it did not stop her from starting a bridging course in June 2012 to eventually get into radiography. Due to needing basic physics and basic anatomy, Jess completed a Certificate IV in Health Science Foundations, so that she could get into university. Jess was on a mission! She went on to complete a Bachelor of Applied Science from Feb-Nov in 2013. She then started a Bachelor of Medical Imaging in February 2014, completing the three-year degree in November 2016.

During the time of her studies Jess continued to work at the salon as a part-time employee and finished her employment at Innovations on December 24th, 2016.

In July of 2021, it was ten years since Jess had her first kidney transplant. The old disease has now gone into the new kidney and over the next couple of years Jess will need to have another kidney transplant. She will be back on dialysis and on the waiting list.

Overall, my time with Jess both personally and professionally has been a journey that I have truly enjoyed, for so many reasons. We have partied, travelled, dined in and out, laughed, cried and learnt so much together and to date I am blessed to spend time with her.

I always love being in her presence and although our plans may chop and change a lot of the time, we eventually always make it work!

Jess, I still see that young, feisty, fearless and courageous woman who I met in 2010! Nothing has changed about you, other than right now you are in full bloom! I am thrilled to share with you that Jess and her partner Luke have a baby on the way due December 2021.

I am so happy for you both and look forward to meeting your bundle of joy!

Love you Jess X

Aunty Cathy is excited beyond words!

INTIMATE MASSAGE

Tammy is a rainbow of colour with a gentle nature about her and someone who talks very openly about everything. Not only is Tammy a client but also a personal friend.

One evening on a night out with mutual friends, Dario, Dawid, Teresa and Hai, Tammy asks if any of us have ever experienced a vaginal massage with a masseuse. I reply, "I didn't even know it was a thing to get a vaginal massage". We all burst into laughter.

Of course, curiosity sets in and we discuss the topic a little further. It became an education lesson about a woman's vulva and I discovered that there are so many reasons why a Yoni massage can be of benefit to women.

Well as it turns out, apparently a 'Yoni Massage' is a professional service that you can book in for or alternately it can be a one-on-one self-service once you master the technique.

They say you learn something new every day and this was certainly no exception!

So who should get a Yoni massage and what exactly does it involve?

It is a lot more detailed than what I could have imagined so I recommend that if you want more clarity on what you may experience with this type of service, do yourself a favour and google search 'Yoni Massage'.

It will be a very interesting and enlightening read to say the least!

LITTLE GIRL LOST

We cannot always predict what may lay ahead but let's be honest, life can be very cruel and tragic at times!

I was only a little girl when my Nonno Lorenzo passed away. For hours on end all that I could hear were the loud voices and hysterical cries that were happening around me. Suddenly a feeling of confusion set in, and my tiny, petite little body froze with stillness.

I sat in the corner of the backyard with my hands forcefully hovering over my tiny face. Trying to block out the noise was difficult and keeping my face covered ensured that I could not see anyone. Feelings of despair, pain and fear engulfed me. Everyone was frantic, it was scary.

What was happening?

I witnessed all this chaos whilst quietly sitting still. Every so often, when it became quiet I would lift my head up to see what everyone was doing. It wasn't long before the screaming would start again, and the echoing cries would become louder and louder. I buried my head into my arms once again, totally still, continuing to sit alone in my own silence!

At such a young age with this first experience of having a loved one pass into the next stage of life, I was mentally scarred. I clearly remember that awful day and have been fearful of death ever since. That very sad day from a long time ago revisits my mind and enters my thoughts, more often than what I would like it to.

For many years I could not comprehend or understand death, but I will always remember how that one horrible and unexpected day made me feel.

Our thoughts and feelings consume us. The circumstances that we face can change our lives in many ways that you just never thought possible. I have come to realise and understand that nothing stays the same forever.

Reality is change is always happening!

LOVE

Unforeseen and overwhelmingly strong are the feelings and emotions that can consume someone in day-to-day life. It is not out of the ordinary to form bonds and connections with certain people in our lifetime and it is no surprise that we encounter and cross paths with special humans that we instantly feel soulfully connected to.

All these experiences for me have been about learning to love, falling in love, expressing love, showing love and in some darker times not loving at all.

As a teenager growing up, I envisaged being a mother and loved the idea. I was in love with my daughter and son way back then, purely in my thoughts before they were even born. This may seem a little out of the ordinary to you as you read this, but it is true!

In 1996 Brooke was born. So delicate and precious, the young girl I had always dreamed of was with me, in real life. In the year of 1999 my son, Corey, arrived early and ready. He was fearless and self-assured.

Brooke and Corey, you will always be my forever loves; a love that is unconditional. Being by your side and watching you grow into young independent adults has been one of the biggest achievements in my life.

My special friendship and relationship with my husband Frank had love sprinkled all over it when we first met. Our relationship was fast, it moved in many different directions and from the very early onset of our courtship it came with no shortage of ongoing challenges. I believe to this day that so much of what we dealt with in our journey together has in many ways been amazing and wonderful, yet also very disheartening and fragile.

Together and in time we grew as a couple. There have been so many ups and downs. At times I have learnt to overlook situations. My intention has been to stay in my comfort zone and look out for the wellbeing of those around me.

Without core deep love, respect and an inner strength that is required for solid and everlasting foundations, it can be somewhat challenging and tiring trying to maintain a healthy and sustainable relationship.

Despite everything we are tackling right now, Frank is one of the most important and special loves of my life. Together we are trying to work through some of our issues in hope that it will lead us to be happier in ourselves and together. Time will tell!

As humans our experiences and circumstances can make us feel distant from one another. In fact, a lot of the time it is when we are living under the same roof. I hear this from others quite often and wonder: Should it be this difficult? Are we supposed to feel like at times we are miles apart on so many levels?

The million-dollar question is, why?

LOVE OF PEOPLE

I often fall in love with people I have crossed paths with. It is a different kind of love. There are people I know and total strangers who I suddenly meet that for some reason catch my attention. Their spirit draws me in, and I find myself falling in love with their substance, the depth of who they are.

For me, these kinds of loves are an expression of kindness we can show towards other people, whether we know them or not. It is a compassionate kind of love. A human quality that inspires and motivates me to genuinely care. Compassionate love is not about intimate desire, either, except perhaps the desire to make the world a better place.

Romantic love, on the other hand, is in many ways very different. For some it may be a fleeting experience of love and for others an eternal love. Falling in love and being in love with someone comes with feelings of intense passion, tenderness, fondness, warmth and a desire for that longing of long-lasting love, a forever love.

I fell in love with the most beautiful soul Ricc who is now a flying angel in heaven. Our love was unconditional and immediate. A different kind of love. A love that comes from a place that deep down in your heart radiates all colours of a rainbow.

Riccstar, I knew I was losing him and without words, without touch, without even any form of physical contact ever again I will always remember and love those road trips during our last summer together. I am in awe of him and everything he shared with me, what he taught me, what I saw, what I gained and what I am still learning and embracing. We will meet again, another place, another lifetime...always and forever very close at heart!

Bella, our family pet who was so much more than I could have ever expected, will live in my heart forever. I fell in love with her, immediately. Bella was and will always be my real treasure. My soft and petite angel Bella is now in heaven back in the arms of Angel Ricc who first placed her in my arms the day she entered our home. What a love! It was extra special.

I have lots of love for Josh, Keanu and Jacko who I have enjoyed watching grow up to be kind-hearted young men. Our family dinners are always interesting whenever these guys are around.

Josh, you are more than you know and you are so helpful and considerate of others which is a beautiful trait to have.

Keanu, I loved having you live with us for nearly six months as an exchange student from Germany. It was such a special time for us all.

Jackson, although we were not in contact for a while I did not love you any less. I am so happy that we are all reunited once again.

Unbosoming

Most recently there was a 'Kai' kind of love. For whatever reason Corey and Kai crossed paths and I couldn't be happier that they did. Seeing Kai and Bailey losing Mumma Kim was so sad. I was heartbroken for them. I only met with Kim on three occasions and our first hug felt so warm and real. I knew that Kimmie was loving my son as much as I loved hers. I told her the last day I saw her that I would never be Kai's mum but I would always love him and do the best I could as though he was my own. For me that will never change, I meant every word.

Kai, who I love so much, thank you for always being so kind, and grateful. Flying angel 'Mumma Kim' would be more than proud of you and your beautiful brother Bailey.

Learning to love yourself in my experience is first and foremost a very important and special kind of love that contributes to filling your own heart with what it really needs. When my love tank is full, I am at my best to love, help and to support others.

It has taken time to really believe that, but I advocate wholeheartedly for self-love.

Embrace it, find it, feel it.

It is a YOU kind of love!

> "The greatest
> healing therapy is
> friendship and love."
> **Hubert H. Humphrey**

Left Kai, middle Kim, Right Corey

MAGICAL LIQUID

An unexpected diagnosis that came with 20 weeks of therapy in 2021 was something my sister-in-law Daniela was not prepared for. Nevertheless, it wasn't too long before Daniela's head space and train of thought manifested into an abundance of positivity. This was now the beginning of a journey like no other.

Unbosoming

On Tuesday 20th July 2021 I accompanied Daniela and attended a day treatment with her at the Peter Mac centre in the heart of Melbourne. I wanted to explore and learn a little more about Daniela and what she was going through in hope that I could share her story with you.

First and foremost, can I just say that walking into the hospital was like an abundance of purity. Everything seemed so sterile and fresh. At the same time I felt like I was entering into a whirlwind of colour. The artwork all over the walls was just spectacular and seemed so fitting to Daniela, who is one of the most talented and creative artists that I know.

Together we made our way to the treatment room that was vibrant and bright. As I made my way into the room it immediately felt like a relaxing and calming space. I was drawn straight to the big glass window that overlooked our beautiful city of Melbourne that was set in clear daylight at the beginning of a new day.

As I gaze outside I find myself closed in, closed down and closed off to one another. It is currently lockdown 5.0 in Melbourne and Covid-19 is still hovering in July of 2021. No doubt it will be for a long time yet to come! Thankfully today, I can be here supporting my sister-in-law, who is on her own road to recovery.

When we put things into perspective, what Daniela is dealing with certainly outweighs everything when it comes to understanding what really is important. In this moment, my mind screams 'Get fu**ed Covid!'

As we sit in the treatment room we start to chat. Daniela begins to tell me that her mum was diagnosed with breast cancer in the year of 2010. I knew of this but wasn't aware of the similarities that their circumstances entailed. As we chatted a little more it was interesting to hear that both Daniela and her mum had a very similar diagnosis. The cancer that they both had was in the left breast and the lump was the same size and in the same position.

I have no doubt that over the many years with all the funding, new technologies and very clever scientists and doctors, the treatment Daniela is receiving today is so much more advanced. Thank goodness for that. Breast cancer survival rates have improved so much, and I am more than hopeful that Daniela's 'magical liquid' is preparing her for the best years yet!

Daniela went on to tell me that she attended treatment with her mum and watched on, week in week out as her mum's condition went from having cancer to be cancer-free. Daniela also recalls that the treatment room her mum experienced was smaller, a lot more congested and nowhere as vibrant as the beautifully designed Peter Mac Centre.

Finding yourself and releasing what is going on in your mind is such wonderful therapy for many people. I was so happy to hear that Daniela is keeping a journal of her thoughts and reflecting on what is really happening to her, within her and about her!

Regardless of the health recovery spaces that Daniela and her mum spent time in, the most important and best outcome is that they remain cancer-free.

Daniela still has five weeks of treatment to go but I have no doubt that the 'magical liquid' that is travelling through every being of Daniela's body is working its magic to cure, enhance, and enrich her life for the better.

I love you Daniela and appreciate the times I spend with you. I hope that one day your artwork is displayed at Peter Mac as a reminder of the journey you are on and how you have personally dealt with breast cancer.

'Magical Liquid' was inspired by Daniela's zest for life, love and laughter.

ONLY A PHONE CALL AWAY

When I noticed Prue's number come up on my phone unexpectedly whilst I was away on a holiday in Germany I immediately became concerned. When I answered the phone I could sense that Prue was a little hesitant and not her usual self. Then it happened! Prue told me that she was recently diagnosed with breast cancer.

I was shocked and caught off guard. Although our conversation was brief I assured Prue that as soon as I landed back in Melbourne I would make time to visit and check in on her progress.

This chapter in Prue's life began on 14th June 2014 and it was the beginning of more than I ever imagined!

When I arrived home, as promised, I caught up with Prue at the salon. Pino is a supportive husband to Prue and along with their daughter Julia, we collaboratively decided that giving Prue a head shave would be the best option. Considering that treatment would leave Prue with minimal hair, if any, it made sense to prepare Prue for what would lay ahead.

It was an emotionally confronting moment and everyone was sad. One thing I know for sure is that I won't ever forget the attitude that Prue instilled upon us in that moment. She was brave and already thinking a million miles ahead to recovery mode and I just loved her more for that reason. Prue had her end game in sight and the countdown to remission was well on its way before it even began.

I have only ever known Prue to be proactive, focused and determined about everything and have always looked up to her as a mentor, confidante and friend. This diagnosis was not letting her down. Thankfully Pino, the fun-loving joker, who is always a real treat to be around, made the head shave moment light-hearted, to say the least.

Prue went on to have treatment for around 12 months and during that time managed to work and progress both on a personal and professional level. Each week she would drop her wig off at the salon and a team member would wash, treat and style it, perfectly ready for the week ahead. Prue always looked stunning with or without her wig and even though she was battling her own personal health issues, she always looked glamorous!

Each time I saw Prue she was radiating a glow about her that made it seem as though her progress was smooth sailing. Contrary to what I saw on the surface, at times, I could also sense that Prue was feeling vulnerable and emotionally distressed. What I loved most was the way Prue would smile and how she would engage in laughter and banter, making everyone around her feel at ease, although deep down I knew her mind was working overtime.

Despite everything that Prue was going through with treatment and recovery, it was evident that maintaining family, friendships and fun was a priority. I will be forever inspired by Prue and can honestly say that this woman has been one of the most influential people in my life. What started out as a haircut and colour service in the salon more than 32 years ago genuinely blossomed into more than I could have ever imagined.

It is now mid-August of 2021 and Prue is thriving in more ways than one. Professionally she is at the top of her game and on a personal note her two children are happily married. Prue and Pino have also been blessed with two beautiful granddaughters and I couldn't be happier for their family. On a health note, Prue is in remission and thriving, looking 15 years younger than her age! What a woman!

Love you dearly Prue and I am so grateful that we crossed paths. You are more to me than you can imagine. Thank you for everything – and I mean everything!!!

Love Cathy X

NANNA DELANEY

I can recall so many things from my childhood and often think about the many afternoons I spent with my brother Laurie and Nanna Delaney.

Each time we popped in to visit Nanna Delaney I was in awe of her beauty. Her snow-white hair was always neatly tamed, and her lips always looked natural with pastel coloured lipstick tones. To top it off, Nanna Delaney had the most colourful dress sense, and her clothing made her a sight to look at!

Being in her presence and in her home felt like a journey in a delicate fairytale book. It made me want to be with her all the time. When Nanna Delaney spoke, her tone was calming and warm. Learning to display good manners and being respectful was imperative. Nanna Delaney didn't like it if we were being rude and nasty and would explain how important it was to be polite and treat one another with kindness.

If I had to share one thought right now it would be the excitement of sharing afternoon tea together. Nanna Delaney would prepare the table with her fine china, cups and saucers in tow, homemade cakes and biscuits and all the little condiments that made it a real tea party. It was special.

I have such wonderful recollections in my mind of those afternoons and will always remember how it made me feel. Laurie was five years old and I was aged three, but despite our very young age, Nanna Delaney would always treat us like little adults. We were always made to feel welcome, loved and safe.

Being taught basic life skills such as manners and kindness has profoundly impacted my life in the best possible way. I am so grateful to have spent so many beautiful moments with Nanna Delaney. My life has been enriched by her presence and that is just magical.

ROAD TRIP

Weekends away in Albury became an ongoing adventure. I was 19 years old and exploring my way in life with Rose. Together we were having experiences that were fun, exciting, risky and interesting!

Unbosoming

I remember these road trips as though it was only yesterday. I would finish work at the salon each Saturday and have my bags packed ready to take off on our little retreat. Each week Rose and I would take it in turns to drive. This getaway became our regular routine, and we always had the best times.

Every week we went on pub crawls, met people, watched bands, drank lots of beer, smoked 'scoobs' and I met my first boyfriend. The rest is history!

There are so many stories that I can share but the one that will always make us laugh is when we got pulled over by the police on the highway on our way to Albury. We had the 'peddle on the metal' and our speed was a little higher than the legal limit. Enjoying the drive and having a great time listening to music, laughing, and chatting was the only thing on our radar! Before we knew it we had a police car waving us down to pull over on the side of the road. Of course, that is exactly what we did. A police officer proceeds to make his way toward us and as I watch him through the side mirror getting closer to the car I begin to wind down my mirror. He approaches the window and I look up at him and smile. Rose and I then burst into laughter. The policeman also starts laughing. Thankfully the police officer was friendly, open-minded and lenient. We sweet talk our way out of why we were a little over the speed limit and not long after we are on our merry little way to our destination, again laughing hysterically!

> "Well, I always say law was meant to be interpreted in a lenient manner. And that what I try to do, is sometimes I lean to one side of it, sometimes I lean to the other."
> **Irving Ravetch**

Your Stories: Real Names

SELF-ACCEPTANCE IS KEY AND FUNDAMENTAL TO OUR EXISTENCE

I may not have been in Cristian's life from the first day he was born but when I did get to meet him I instantly fell in love. This very special moment came to life just before Cristian turned one.

Not long after meeting Cristian he came into the salon and I gave him his first haircut. He sat in the chair and did not flinch. We have photos of that very day and as a 12-year-old now, he still maintains a stylish, well-presented look, with neat and tidy locks.

Nothing has changed over the years other than I love him even more. I am always enlightened and entertained whenever I am in his presence, and his banter, conversations and eccentric little personality is truly infectious!

Communicating with Cristian is like talking to an older, mature and worldly man who is not afraid to have a voice. His views and opinions often make a lot of sense, and he is not backwards in coming forward when he needs to be heard!

When we get together for a catch up, Cristian will always have lovely, manicured fingernails. The colours on his nails will vary from bold and bright to glossed up with natural tones that look delicate and subtle. The shape of his nails are beautifully mastered and every so often his lashes are long and lush and his lips are enhanced with gloss.

Clothing and fashion is of interest to Cristian. Labels and brands including Gucci, Louis Vuitton, Balenciaga, Prada and Versace amongst others, are just some of the high-end brands that Cristian loves and I always tell him how lucky he is to be gifted with such expensive items.

I personally don't own any of these expensive labels unless they were purchased on one of my travels to Bali. Regardless of the cost, I love my goods and enjoy utilising them the same.

For Cristian, sporting a 'Gucci' bag, the real deal, is what he loves and when getting ready to go on an outing, rest assured he will be embracing his little bag with pride and joy.

Another love of Cristian's is walking a parade of showcasing high heels and his mum's clothing. These moments are always enjoyable to watch. On one occasion in Rosebud, when Cristian was six, he asked if he could play dress ups. Brooke and I let Cristian do his thing and we invited him to explore our wardrobe of clothing. I have a collection of images with Cristian all dolled up from his fashion shows and no doubt will share them with him, all in good time!

If there is one thing I can confidently tell you about Cristian, it is that he is a food connoisseur. A combination of flavours including Italian, Malaysian, Vietnamese, Portuguese, Cantonese, Japanese, Korean, Modern, Chinese and Mexican are some of the many cuisines that Cristian is well educated about. He is culturally experienced in many flavours of the world and when dining out together, it is so good just letting him order for the table. He knows exactly what he is doing! Cristian is also a whiz in the kitchen. He is very resourceful in exploring recipes, takes time to source out interesting produce and will not shy away from ingredients that we would not usually have in the pantry. Best of all, his artistic detail to presentation on delivery to the table has a flair to it that makes you feel in awe of what he has just cooked up!

Aside from food, Cristian is also very much a car enthusiast. He loves Ferrari, Lamborghini, Maserati, Tesla, Mercedes, BMW, Aston Martin, Porsche and Fiat. Models, motors, gears, speed, shape and size, you name it, he knows about it!

One afternoon mid-year in 2020, Cristian and I went for a walk to visit his Nonno and Nonna. Together interlocking arms and elbows and with his little Gucci bag accompanying him, Cristian and I set off for our adventure. Cristian loves a chat and enjoys discussions about many different topics which makes our conversations always so interesting. As we kept walking, we continued to discuss relationships and the importance of self-identity. It was so endearing to hear such a young person speak so articulately about his individuality. Cristian you are truly someone special!

For a 12-year-old, Cristian is certainly a person who doesn't hold back in sharing his thoughts, feelings, views and ideas. I really believe that young people are forced to learn things much earlier than they need to, and just like Cristian, they are being tested. Although Cristian may be young in age, I think that being a witness to a diverse set of circumstances has in many ways fine-tuned him into a bold, determined and very special individual. He is certainly someone who I adore and love, immensely.

In his own right, Cristian continues to grow into a soulful human being with an abundance of depth and substance about him and is flourishing, beautifully.

Cristian has a heart of gold.

SHAPING FUTURES, PHILIPPINES – GETTING SOMETHING STARTED

As my journey into a National Training Centre and visiting an SOS orphanage in the Philippines began to take place, I knew that giving something of myself was the only way to keep moving forward in my life.

'Shaping Futures' is a Schwarzkopf initiative with the purpose of training and educating young people the skills of hairdressing, in the Philippines. This was the beginning of something I could have never imagined! It made me want to open my mind to understand the life of others through their eyes. I was excited, overwhelmed and felt blessed.

It was in 2015 when a new life experience gave me so much joy. I was enlightened by the most precious souls who embraced every opportunity to learn and took nothing for granted. I loved everything about 'Shaping Futures' and was so lucky to be able to return in 2016 and 2017. Participating once again and helping to mentor young people was truly amazing. I will always have the fondest of memories of my time in the Philippines.

Everyone who has ever volunteered with 'Shaping Futures' worldwide would agree how special it is to be involved. I worked with such wonderful people who shared the same vison and met the loveliest families at the training centre and in the villages who looked after us, like family. There was never a shortage of karaoke sessions, laughter, and there was always an abundance of smiles each day. Whatever these families could offer it was shared with open arms. The gift of giving was everywhere!

I was privileged to be a part of this initiative for three years in a row and am so happy the Schwarzkopf family took me under their wing! In return they gave me wings of my own with which to fly and I am so thankful that they did!

It was here that I crossed paths with Dario, a hairdresser and volunteer who was also from Melbourne. He enhanced my life in so many ways. Over time our friendship blossomed, and our conversations continued to flourish. Thank you for everything Dario and for entrusting me with your first visit into our family home. Sometimes business and pleasure do go hand in hand and on this occasion, it naturally did. I truly love you Dario and we will always be your surrogate family!

Spending time with such humble and gentle souls has enriched my life. I am blessed to have been able to be part of Shaping Futures in the Philippines. A lifetime of memories that have found a place in my heart forever.

Thank you to all the students for sharing and giving something of yourselves and allowing me to be a part of your lives. I will be forever grateful.

Volunesia
(noun)

that moment when you forget you're
volunteering to help change lives,
because it's changing yours…

Shaping Future Trainees
Volunteers: Katherine, Cathy, Vera, Sian, Dario

SWEET THING

During the first ISO lockdown in March 2020 I decided to close the salon for a month as we were entering uncharted territories and I needed to just breathe, slow down and think. For some reason this time spent at home prompted me to start planning house renovations, something I had wanted to do for such a long time but had never found time for.

In the same month, Friday 6th March 2020 we had to say goodbye to our family pet dog 'Bella' who became unwell in unexpected circumstances. We were all devastated and could not believe what lay ahead of us. I put on my purple scarf and made my way to the Vet Clinic and Hospital in Bundoora where Bella was under observation and receiving treatment.

Ricc's favourite colour was purple, and I felt that Bella was going to be with him soon.

Once I was told the awful news, I immediately called Frank, Brooke and Corey. Everyone left work early on that Friday so that we could gather as a family and be with our baby Bella. One by one we held Bella and said our last goodbye. Brooke and I shared a special moment to gently wrap the purple scarf around Bella. We kissed her, held her and Bella peacefully fell asleep, forever. It was sudden and something we weren't prepared for. We were all heartbroken and devasted!

I didn't sleep that night and was feeling so many different emotions. I felt empty and scattered! My mind was in overdrive, and something came over me. I was feeling a little lost and so much was going on that I needed a distraction, something to give me a brighter focus, a sense of purpose.

I got up early that morning and decided to start painting the house. Frank was a little dazzled at my urgency to get this happening but nevertheless, off we went to the paint store to begin choosing colours. It felt a little overwhelming looking at white colour swabs that looked so alike. How hard could it really be to pick a white wall colour for a home? We were in the paint store no more than ten minutes and although people advised me to get some samples to try out, in that moment when I spotted a white colour named 'Sweet thing' the decision was made. "That's it, no trials, no samples, this is the colour."

My princess Bella was the 'sweetest thing' ever; so adorable, precious and delicate. I was so in love with her that I wanted her presence always to remain in our family home and so just like that 'Sweet thing' came to light.

We will always be embraced by Bella knowing that our home makeover was inspired because of her gentle nature, natural beauty and serene personality.

TUESDAY TREATS

During midyear lockdown in 2020 whilst home doing renovations through my love of music, another journey in my life began to take shape. 'Tuesday Treats' was born when touching base and checking in on my friend Marcus. We agreed that each week on a Tuesday we would send each other a song and I would add it to the playlist. I then thought whoever I happen to call or whoever may call me in that first week, I would invite them to become a part of this collaboration of music.

I was surprised with the amazing diversity of music and tunes that came together. Without a doubt, the sounds, vibes and tunes were so very different, but to me relatable.

In those moments of exchanging songs, we may have felt happy, sad, lonely, vulnerable, excited, anxious, confident, confused, energetic and even in a party mood, but whatever it was for each of us, all those different emotions, feelings and thoughts, I felt the love shared through the power of music.

Heartfelt thanks to these beautiful people, Marcus, Carl, Brooke, Jess, Samantha, Tammy and Dario who in one way or another have influenced and enhanced my life. You are all dear to my heart and I look forward to when we can gather to listen to this playlist and enjoy being in the presence of one another.

For me, love of music fills my heart soulfully.
I need music, especially when I work.
Music grounds me.
It is pure emotion and I need that extension.

"If you don't like the
world you're living in,
Take a look around you,
at least you got friends"
-PRINCE, "Let's go crazy"

Unbosoming

Spotify playlist **'Tuesday Treats'**

Marcus - Tuesday Treats
Carl - Wednesday Worldwide
Brooke - Thursday Thoughts
Jess - Friday Feels
Samantha - Sassy Saturday
Tammy - Smooth Sunday
Dario - Monday Moves
Cathy - Weekly Wonders

TURNING POINT

The early days, being of Italian background and growing up in the Craigieburn community with mostly Australians, was a time of fruitful learning about other cultures and families. My bestie Bushells and her family became like my family and my family became her family. I experienced my first Aussie roast at her house and was always so excited to have sweets after dinner because that just was not a tradition in my house growing up. It was a real treat for me.

I loved Bushells and her family and she was always excited to have dinner at mine, indulging in Mum's pasta and meatballs! Our families got along well and that made our time together easy and comfortable. Bushell's parents loved a bevvy or three and so did my dad. The Aussies were beer drinkers and my Italian dad was a homemade wine lover.

Bushells and I witnessed some funny afternoon bevvy sessions growing up and I often wonder if that's why I love a Sunday session so much?

Bushells and I practically lived at the tennis courts along with my brother and many other local kids from the community. We spent so many hours training, leisurely playing or just hanging out.

I always dreamt of getting my name engraved on one of the championship boards in the tennis room clubhouse and at the age of 15 managed to have that happen. I won the girls' Junior Club Championship, playing in the final against my bestie Bushells.

All those years spent at the courts practising and Saturday morning competitions also led me to an opportunity of representing Victoria in the Junior Shell Squad. I will always be grateful to my mum who drove all over the place so that I could be a part of that team. Love you Mum, more than you can ever imagine!

As much as I loved tennis at the age of 15, I was disliking school and always in trouble. I came home after Year 10 and told my parents I was not going back to do Year 11. The deal was that if I found an apprenticeship or a job then I could leave school and follow my passion for hairdressing.

I would often practise cutting and colouring hair at home without my mum knowing. Then one day my sister Luci came out of the bathroom with what we call a 'forehead basher fringe'. It is the fringe that is so short that all you see is a forehead! Well I didn't know what a cowlick was back then!

Now in my 50s, I love sporting a fringe. A Dario speciality!

The trials and tribulations of practising hairdressing prior to a lot of training saw Lozza end up with a cut ear, orange hair, yellow tips and he even entertained the idea of getting a perm.

Michelle, my youngest sister, was only five at the time, but I always remember her following me around and watching everything I did. It is not surprising that Michelle grew up to be one of the most creative and naturally talented team members at the salon. Her passion and skills earned her a positive reputation and strong following within the community of Craigieburn and during her time at the salon Michelle was fortunate to win an Indola Hairdressing competition at Sydney Hair Expo. The winning prize of travelling to London provided her with an opportunity to travel abroad, which she did with her then boyfriend, salon client and now husband Lee.

My niece Briana has the same natural hairdressing talent, and I was also blessed to have taken her under my wing to complete her hairdressing apprenticeship at Innovations. Briana was nominated as Apprentice of the Year in 2018 and was announced the winner at the awards evening, a recognition well deserved.

I love Mum and Dad for supporting my dream to become a hairdresser and for embracing the Bushells family, and many of the other neighbours and families in our community.

Most importantly, they gave me the freedom to be me!

YARRA ON THE WATER

Holidaying in Yarrawonga with the Vescio, Mercuri, and Perrone families, amongst others, has been a yearly destination for more than 20 years. Watching the sun go down and sitting on the green grass underneath the most beautiful big tree has been a treat. We are so lucky for all the memories we have made together and I look forward to being able to travel there again once we have the freedom to do so.

Your Stories: Real Names

Melbourne Cup long weekend in Yarra is a haven of relaxation, family, friends, fun and laughter. We have enjoyed boat cruises, jet ski rides and have been entertained in more ways than one.

We have an allocated cooking agenda, and it works perfectly. We revisit the same shopping list and tweak it a little each year to suit us. Depending on how many will be holidaying in Yarrawonga that year will determine the quantity of food. Despite the menu changes, it is essential that Sunday salsa is my husband's job. He never disappoints with his yummy meatballs and his pasta sauce. Always on point!

We have had more than 15 people share the apartment over one weekend and whether you are bunking with someone, pulling out a sofa bed or sleeping on a blow-up mattress, it all works well. It is one big slumber party.

Music, dancing, floorshows, barbeques, dress ups and wine o'clock time is happening throughout our time there! It is an awesome getaway and we have had some amazing moments and experiences that no doubt we all cherish.

Afternoon siesta and doing a whole lot of 'fu** all' is what we enjoy and sitting on our front porch is the ideal spot to sit back and let time just drift away.

Take us back to Yarra so that we can house hop and visit our friends for a well overdue catch up. Whether it is in their abode or out under the tree, I love it!

Unbosoming

WHITE SWAN

I do not think I really accepted or understood death until Ricc passed away.

In 2010 the last 12 months of Ricc's life was a journey like no other. He taught me so much and the time we spent together is priceless, to say the least.

It was magical to spend these precious moments with Ricc. He would often console me about him moving on in to the next chapter of his life. He would always tell me not to be sad, not to cry and that he would be just fine as he had courageously accepted that he was dying. He just wanted to make the most of the time he had left.

We certainly did have some truly special get togethers, often just the two of us. They are memories that are always close to my heart.

One day he caught me by surprise and asked me what animal I would like to come back as in my next life. I did not answer immediately because I was pondering my reply. He then popped up and said, "I am coming back as a white swan". I swiftly replied, "Of course, yes, how beautiful, serene, fluffy and soft, just like you". What a moment. It still gives me goose bumps now!

For a long time after his passing, I was always on the lookout for a white swan, but I never did see one until seven years later.

A family emergency called for me to travel to London and within less than 12 hours I left on a one-way ticket! I went to rescue my daughter who was very unwell whilst living overseas and it was a very confronting and frightening time for us both. Hospital visits, doctors, getting answers and trying to understand a medical condition called vestibular neuritis. Everything was so overwhelming and daunting.

The challenge of getting her home was unsettling and we needed medical approval to travel. This made our situation even more challenging. All I knew was that my mission was to somehow get back home to Australia together.

One beautiful sunny day in London I was taking a walk through Hyde Park with Brooke and just in front of us a white swan appeared. My first words to Brooke were "Ricc is here". It may sound bizarre or out of the ordinary but I followed that swan around the lake and kept positive thoughts in my head. I was talking to the swan as though I was talking to Ricc. I felt elated, I smiled, I was happy. I knew in that moment what had to be done. I knew everything was going to work out.

I believe that telling little white lies can and will come into play when necessary. Sometimes you need to be your own saviour and when it matters most do what you need to do!

My plan came to life on day eight of being in London and by day ten we were in the air flying, making our way home.

There was no way my daughter would have made it back alone. If you ever get a sudden call of emergency, near or far, do what you need to do, whether it's family or not. I would hate to imagine what would have been if I had not gone to London. Clearly that was never going to be the case!

And for the record, my beautiful daughter is doing well. Her health has improved so much, and I am forever grateful to all her London

Unbosoming

family, especially Rach, Gabe and Will amongst others for being there by her side.

Your support ensured that Brooke was never alone, and I will be forever thankful.

I love you all so much XXX.

CHAPTER 3

Your Stories: Danger, Manipulation and Bad Attitudes

LEADERSHIP UNDER THE RADAR

Miss Mazza was never going to get a higher position at work. It was clear that the many years spent dedicating herself to supporting the needs of others was overlooked on numerous occasions.

At this workplace it was the two senior leaders, Mr Trauler and Mrs Scusini, who often made snide remarks about Miss Mazza. They would undermine and overlook her ideas and they would often agree that Miss Mazza was a drainer! Mr Trauler and Mrs Scusini would sit in their office behind closed doors, coffee in hand and share in their own jokes and laughter at the expense of not only Miss Mazza but other members of the staff.

Unbosoming

I have been a hairdresser to both Miss Mazza and Mrs Scusini for many years. What I always found to be most interesting was the two very different sides of the conversations that were shared with me regarding their workplace.

I came to realise that Mrs Scusini was exceptional at flying under the radar and I witnessed this type of behaviour quite frequently. It was interesting to hear what others would say about staff members within this workplace. It made for interesting listening to say the least. At times I would see these staff members all together and it was as though not a bad word ever came out of Mrs Scusini's mouth. When you witnessed her communicating with her colleagues, no one would have known any different other than what they witnessed about her on the surface.

Although Miss Mazza had so much to offer the workplace it was evident that she was never going to be placed in a more influential and leading role. Miss Mazza had been a dedicated and committed employee of her workplace for more than a decade and those in authoritarian roles often thought that she was a whinger. They found her to be annoying and brushed off her ideas time and time again.

When you have great content and you share your thoughts in meetings with colleagues only to have your input overlooked or shut down, eventually as a person you begin to lose your enthusiasm towards what you were once passionate about.

I believe in time Miss Mazza started to read between the lines a little more and could sense that certain people worked together in ways that would clearly only benefit themselves. Mr Trauler and Mrs Scusini flew under the radar a lot. In front of her face, they acted in one way whilst behind her back they were making jokes at her expense. I clearly knew this was the case because quite frankly Mrs Scusini would often fill me in about the people who pissed her off and the conversation was not always just about Miss Mazza.

It was difficult knowing what I knew. I thought it was a pretty fu**ed up scenario that both Mr Trauler and Mrs Scusini, the two people in leadership roles, often wished Miss Mazza would leave the workplace. It was very clear that Miss Mazza was never going to be able to work her way up to the top as it was evident the wall had been built a long time ago and there was no climbing over it for her.

I was glad when Miss Mazza decided to make the move to a new workplace that would challenge her and more importantly, where she would be appreciated.

Miss Mazza is truly a genuine and kind-spirited person. To have the courage to decide to leave a workplace after so many years is a big step. Taking the initiative to move on was clearly in her best interest.

When I see Miss Mazza now at the salon I can sense a relaxed and chilled presence within her. I listen to what she tells me about her new work environment, her colleagues and the community, and I feel empowered by her stories.

Being valued and appreciated in our workplace is important.

Being happy can make a huge difference in our daily life.

Whatever it may be that you are doing, hopefully you will make the right decision so you can have success in your chosen field. Do what is best for you!

MONEY MATTERS

There was something way too nice about Raja. I picked it from the day we met and just could not put my finger on it. I would often say to one of my employees that something did not feel quite right about Raja and my colleague would respond with, "Oh you're overthinking it, she's just happy and friendly".

As time went on occasionally Raja would gift us with little treats and would often go out of her way to be super nice, but I would always be sceptical. A few months went by when I started to notice that money was going missing from my wallet on a weekly basis and at times on a daily basis. I actually started querying myself and thinking that I must have spent more money on shopping or perhaps I thought I had money when in fact maybe I didn't.

Out of the blue a couple of other staff members had mentioned they had money missing from their personal bag. We were all questioning ourselves and wondering how this was possible. There was no way we could all have money disappearing week after week with no accountability for where it is. Where was our money going?

As time went on, we came to realise that something just didn't seem right. We all felt uncomfortable about what was happening, and it began to feel a little eerie around Raja.

In my thoughts I was feeling confident that Raja was the salon thief and so I set out a plan to bait her. The thought of someone stealing and a sense of betrayal within my workplace felt pretty fu**ed up.

I didn't mention anything to any of the employees about my plan as I wanted concrete evidence before shedding any light on this situation. It was not fair to point the finger at anyone but deep down I knew something was wrong and my intuition did not let me down. This scenario was no exception.

One Friday evening I put $70 in my wallet. The following morning, we all arrived to work, had our usual coffee catch up and then opened the salon doors at 8am ready for a busy Saturday morning. By 9.10am the $70 was gone! Remaining composed and calm was a real effort for me. We had another five hours of work time before the salon closed for the day so making small talk and acting normal was fu**ing pissing me off, especially knowing what just happened. Thank fu** for the end of the day!!

After work we all stayed back as we usually do to have a coffee and chat but, on this day, I was desperate for everyone to leave! Finally, everyone was ready to go home for the weekend and I made my way back into the salon. After reviewing the footage I found exactly what I needed! The camera did not lie.

Within hours I was at my ex-employee's front door with my sister alongside me. It was not too long before a confession had been made and her husband became aware of what his wife had been up to.

Fast forward three months and I get a phone call from a salon owner who was now the employer of my ex-employee. And what do you know? Raja was up to her old tricks, stealing money again.

NASTY

Alexis and Buffy have been besties for years. They would often keep each other company whilst getting their hair done at the salon and seemed to be more like sisters than just friends. I had known them both for about five years and also knew their families reasonably well. At the age of 16 they seemed energetic, fun loving and full of life! I had never really known Alexis or Buffy to have a bad bone in their body, they seemed so nice all the time and then just like that, unexpectedly, things went terribly wrong! Enjoying teenage years and high school experiences with your bestie is usually a blast, it should be awesome, right?

Alexis and her boyfriend were really happy in their newfound romance. I liked Alexis and her attitude towards life. Each time she visited the salon we would chat about all sorts of topics and her presence was always calming and pleasant. On one of the salon visits Alexis came alone and I began to get the impression something was wrong. Alexis seemed really upset and proceeded to tell me how angry she was with Buffy. Buffy had made a decision that went horribly wrong. Her motives were somewhat disturbing, and her attitude became nasty!

As Alexis kept talking to me I could see the tears rolling down her face. She went on to explain what happened.
"One random day in the school yard at lunchtime, Buffy started questioning me about my boyfriend Tanner and was becoming really aggressive towards me. All the other students were around us watching and listening. Buffy began belittling and undermining me in front of everyone. I tried to stand up for myself and then Buffy started yelling out in front of everyone that I was a slut and that I sucked di** for money!"

As Alexis kept explaining this awful scenario to me she was crying hysterically and was so upset.

Danger, Manipulation and Bad Attitudes

As it turned out Buffy liked Tanner and was jealous of the relationship Alexis had with him. Apparently, Buffy also kept prank calling Tanner and leaving nasty messages about Alexis.

The drama and hostility between the girls got out of hand and within a few hours of the incident happening, the girls' parents were informed. Buffy and Alexis never rekindled their friendship.

A few weeks after this altercation between the girls, Alexis decided to change high schools. Within six months her and her family moved out of Craigieburn.

When you read this story so many of you may relate to it or know someone who has been in a similar situation. These types of unwarranted and uninvited behaviours are happening in schools and within our communities. So many young people are affected by experiences just like this and it can have damaging effects on one's health and wellbeing.

Primary and secondary school years can be challenging. As you get older and share different experiences with all types of people, you soon come to realise some friendships will come and go quite easily, whereas some are there to stay and grow.

Remember that relationships are a two-way partnership.

Be the kind of friend that you would like to have.

Have a voice and let others know when their behaviour is unacceptable and unwarranted.

Sometimes we need to step out of our comfort zone and act!

Unbosoming

PAYBACK

It was a normal busy Saturday morning in the salon and I was giving Jarvie his monthly haircut. He was well-known within the community and was a self-assured man in his early 20s. On this particular day, Jarvie seemed a little rattled and something was not right. I didn't think much of it and just let him keep talking, as he always did.

He was a man of many words and ran on adrenaline. I kept listening to Jarvie and the conversation, and as per usual it was about gangs, drugs and rivalries. As he was chatting he kept sipping on his energy drink and talking at the speed of a hundred miles an hour. This was not unusual for him.

If there was any given time that I witnessed an instant reaction that caught me off guard, it was this very moment! Jarvie read a text message from his phone and simultaneously someone was ringing him. Within a second Jarvie sprung out of the chair, ripped the cutting cape off from around his neck and ran out of the salon front door. He gained the attention from others in the salon who questioned, "Oh my god what was that about? What just happened? Where did he go?" I proceeded to sweep up the hair from the floor and cleaned up my workstation.

Whilst I was waiting, not knowing if Jarvie would return, I heard loud noises coming from outside. There was not anything in my direct vision although there were loud sounds of roaring motorbikes.

Within ten minutes Jarvie casually walked back into the salon and sat in the same chair. I asked him if everything was okay and he just smiled at me and replied, "Fu**en oath, it was payback time, all good now". Jarvie then requested that I hurry up and finish off the haircut, of which I did, and then off he went again.

Our end of day was nearing, and I had half an hour to spare before closing. All the team were wanting a snack so I got my bag and went for a walk. As I was approaching the local shop around the corner I could see lots of people gathered around. There seemed to be a lot of noise and commotion going on and the closer I got the more I could see. There was shattered glass all over the floor and what seemed to look like a big wooden stick.

Santana, a local store owner, and her co-worker, looked distressed, yelling questions about what had just happened. I asked them if they were okay. They didn't say too much.

What I did see were two people with pale white faces, in shock. Within minutes the police were in sight, the roar of the motorbikes had disappeared, and damage had been done.

When I saw Jarvie a month later he filled me in on what happened. In simple terms, Jarvie explained the situation to be "an eye for an eye". Drugs, money, power and payback.

As we get older many people influence our way of thinking, our attitudes, our values and our behaviours. While some of these people may be important in our development, their influences are not always in our best interest. Understand and know the risks involved in what you are doing. Know that your choices can be different from others and make decisions that will not put yourself or others in harm's way.

PRICE TAG

When Prinnie sat in the salon chair the first thing she told me was that her debutante dress cost $5000. I replied, "Wow, really, I only spent $100 on my daughter's deb dress! And my wedding dress cost me $900." If there is one thing I know for sure it is that I am a bargain hunter when it comes to clothing. I have never been into spending big dollars on an outfit, unless it's an item on the sale rack. That is just me!

On the day of Prinnie's debutante, all I can say is "what a fu**ing nightmare". A miserable presence was clearly evident. The salon staff were all witnesses to her negative attitude and the bitching about everything was draining, to say the least.

This day was supposed be a special time, a wonderful occasion in her life, yet the topic of conversation was about the other girls and how they would look. Prinnie was hungry for attention, and in my thoughts was clearly going the wrong way about it! All she kept repeating was, "I better look the best".

To top it off her mum Talulah wasn't making the situation any better. Her input into the conversation was even worse and it felt as though her daughter was entering a beauty pageant and the claws were out! Nasty!

We seriously couldn't wait for them to exit the salon that day!

My mum would say it didn't matter what you wore. If you were comfortable and happy with how it looked and how it made you feel, then it was good enough. I totally agree! To date, I still have clothing that I mix and match with other wardrobe items and believe it's important to embrace your own identity when it comes to fashion and styling.

There will always be people around us who love expensive purchases whatever that may entail and that's completely fine. I just do not think that you need to keep up with others. Live within your means and never doubt that you will look just as beautiful in a bargain buy outfit, the one you can afford.

Feeling good about yourself outweighs any dollar value and amount of money you have spent on your clothes!

> "There is no beauty in the finest cloth if it makes hunger and unhappiness."
> **Mahatma Gandhi**

SNEAKY

Independence and self-discovery are journeys that can travel in many directions!

If you are a person who is dependent on the opinions of others to validate who you really are and what you're thinking, let me tell you, it's a recipe for disaster.

When I first met Houston I thought he was a good guy. His mannerisms were polite, and I always felt comfortable around him. On the contrary, Houston's sister Theodora was a bitch, a nasty woman who smiled from ear to ear but underlying was a person who could manipulate a situation very quickly to suit herself!

Unbosoming

The more I got to know Houston the better I felt about him. He was a great guy and a big kid at heart. What surprised me the most was when I saw Houston and Theodora together, it felt like I was witnessing a different man. Who was he?

Theodora seemed to have a hold on Houston, and it really bothered me that she was able to override his conversations and just take over in a way that made him seem vulnerable, withdrawn and sad. Each time I spoke with Houston, his story was repetitive, consuming and tiresome. He looked completely drained and deflated. The cycle of manipulation that Houston was experiencing was so noticeable that I often wondered why he could not read between the lines himself!

I would spend hours in the salon with Theodora during her appointments and the whole time she would bad mouth her network of 'so called friends'. Theodora was self-centred, spoilt and bossy. It is no surprise that her behaviour displayed a lot of toxicity. I always thought of Theodora as a delusional person who thought she was better than everyone else. Her power trips never intimidated me. On the contrary I would laugh inside and would always think, "This fu**er thinks I am sweet bait or a dumb arse that doesn't know any better!"

I would literally see Theodora days later at a sporting event and sure enough she was flying under the radar and friendly with everyone. Hahaha, besties with all the people she bagged out to me! Go figure? Knowing what I knew, honestly, I really enjoyed watching Theodora act like everyone's bullshit friend. I found it to be very superficial.

As time went on Theodora continued to master every situation in a way that had most people blind-sided. I continued to witness Theodora's insincerity each time we crossed paths at the salon or out in the community, and honestly, I loathed her. She was yuck!

Danger, Manipulation and Bad Attitudes

Theodora's nasty words and controlling actions towards her brother were unacceptable. Her manipulation and awful mannerisms towards Houston over and over were becoming a very tiring experience to witness. Each time Houston vented his concerns to me I could see him becoming more depressed and after many years and a lot of feedback from Houston, I decided it was time to put this shit to rest.

In true form Theodora stayed on par with her bitchy personality. I think that deep down Houston learnt from a young age that it's unrealistic to like and respect everyone, especially when you have been mistreated the way he had been. For some reason though he just did not have the courage to confront his sister about how she made him feel.

If you're honest you would agree that we all have people in our lives that you just need to move on from, let that fu**er go and fu** right off!

The truth is, I was actually happy to get Theodora off my client list. As a business owner and hairdresser to Theodora I knew it was time to confront this nasty mole. I didn't want her to enter my salon ever again. Her bullshit needed to be put to bed and her mouth needed shutting up. When you keep coming at me with a story repeatedly that has no truth or substance to it, eventually I will call it out.

With Houston's blessing to call his sister's shit out, I did exactly that.

I contacted Theodora and asked to meet up for a chat. We met at a local coffee shop and our conversation lasted no more than ten minutes. The confrontation with Theodora went down reasonably well. I was polite, professional and honest. I informed Theodora that her obnoxious and nasty conversations about everyone, including her family were bringing an element of negativity into my workplace.

I proceeded to tell her that my staff and I didn't enjoy her presence in the salon and in a nutshell I requested that she find another salon to look after her hair and beauty needs.

Theodora left before her latte arrived and I sat back and enjoyed my long macchiato. I felt a sense of freedom. I did what was right for me, my team and my workplace.

On the way home I rang Houston and told him what had just happened. We had a good chat about a lot of things, and I encouraged him to keep staying true to himself. I came to realise that if Houston started to believe in himself a little more and stopped listening to Theodora maybe his life would turn around for the better.

The best and most important lesson I learnt from these two siblings is that although they came from the same parents, I saw one as a colourful rainbow and the other a cloud of darkness, literally!

On a more positive note, Houston is now 35 years old and has been married for three years to Avalon, who I have known for many years. What a gorgeous couple! He is still a beautiful soul and is not in contact with his sister and hasn't been for more than eight years.

Respect yourself and others but remember that if you are not being treated in a kind and safe manner by a family member or a friend, think about what actions you can take to improve your circumstances. Try to build confidence in yourself and make decisions that feel right for you!

CHAPTER 4

Your Stories: Mental Health and Addiction

ALCOHOLICS ANONYMOUS

It was definitely an eye-opener to sit around a table with a group of people who all had a story to share. I was asked by my client Joye if I would like to support her and attend an AA (Alcoholics Anonymous) meeting. Yes, I had no hesitation. Of course I would be by her side.

The meetings were held on a Monday night and together we made our way to what was one of the most awakening experiences ever. Meeting all these people was so interesting. We were all aged between 18 and 70, came from all walks of life, had diverse backgrounds and cultures and our family dynamics were very different. Everyone was so nice and so friendly. We were made to feel welcome and included from day one, and each week thereafter.

When I started to listen to everyone sharing their reasons for attending AA meetings, it made me realise how important it was to each of these individuals to be present amongst others who were also experiencing difficulties in their lives. It made me realise how much self-reflection is needed to acknowledge a problem. This requires one's inner strength and courage to show up and be accountable. These people made it evident at these meetings.

Each week when I attended the meetings with Joye it was so different. The mood varied depending on what people were openly expressing and from a moment of tears to a moment of laughter, emotions were constantly being released. Every person had a lot going on in their life. I could not only see the vulnerability and anxiety of others right in front of me, but I could feel it too! For me personally, I wanted to continue to listen and learn more. The time I spent at the AA meetings was enlightening and very confronting!

Some people go through so much and I understand we all have choices in life, but I can also understand why reaching out for alcohol, drugs or prescription medication to shut off your reality is what can happen. The trauma, sadness and danger people had been exposed to was intense, and the real emotions and rawness of what was being spoken about was clear at every meeting.

Each week I continued to listen to Joye communicate her story and felt so proud of her. The way she conducted herself and the stories she shared were a positive way for her to better understand herself and the concerns of her family.

The road trips to the meetings every Monday gave us time to talk about many things. This experience made a difference in each of our lives. As the support person, I learnt from Joye and together we appreciated everything we both learnt from these AA meetings.

I would encourage others who are facing difficulties to reach out to get the help they need. Whether you are speaking to a family member, friend, work colleague or seeking professional guidance, assistance is available.

It is 'only always' your choice as an individual to make changes in your life.

Don't underestimate what may be possible! Reach out to others for support.

We all need it sometimes.

AWAKENING

When Penelope walked into the salon in an emotional and distraught manner I thought one of her family members had been badly injured or passed away. I immediately took Penelope out to the back room and asked her what had happened.

Penelope replied with, "I'm not a hypocrite. I loved that guy Ricc who worked here at your salon. I know he was gay and I was fine with that. My son has just 'come out' and told me he is gay and I'm not coping. What is everyone going to think about my son and my family now?"

Unbosoming

I put my arms around Penelope and asked her to calm down. I then told her that it doesn't matter what everyone else thinks about her son Jasper and that her son needs his mum right now more than ever before.

Although Penelope was listening I knew her thoughts didn't align with mine and that's okay. I did go on to tell Penelope that I couldn't keep going with the conversation and that I wasn't the right person to support her as this was an issue that I felt strongly about. Having grown up with gay family members and friends I couldn't understand Penelope and her concerns. For me this moment felt sad and I was disheartened because I have always valued a person not for their sexual preferences but simply as a person. I just didn't understand.

Before we went back into the salon I told Penelope that there was a good chance that she would lose her son. Without family support it would be extremely difficult and confronting for Jasper to feel confident and self-assured, especially if he wasn't going to be accepted by his own family.

Not too long after Jasper 'came out' to his family about his sexuality, he moved out of the family home. For many years Jasper faced numerous personal setbacks that made him feel lonely, isolated, sad and rejected.

I am so happy to share with you that after a period of time Penelope and her family became more open-minded about Jasper's sexuality and as a family they rekindled their relationship.

I always have and always will advocate to support the LGBTQ Community...after all, 'Love is love irrespective of your choice of who you love'.

Mental Health and Addiction

BAKED

Annabelle, a salon client who I became friends with a very long time ago, was a free-spirited person who was living on the edge. It was as though she didn't have a care in the world. Nothing seemed to bother Annabelle and the group of friends that we hung out with. The more I got to know her and her friends, the more aware I became. Everyone was extremely diverse, and, in many ways, I continued to learn.

When I first started hanging out with them I was a little naïve in some ways, or maybe I tried to act naïve to protect myself. A lot of the time when we hung out together I was not sure what a day would entail and how the night would end.

It was not too long before I had my eyes wide open and was learning about life from many different scenarios that I found myself in. Put it this way, I needed to be alert, to say the least!

I decided one day when Annabelle and crew were in baking mode that I would try the hash brownies they had just made. I was about 19 years old at the time and had never been interested in experimenting with what looked like a chocolate brownie so when Annabelle said, "I made hash brownies and they are on point, here, have some and try them out", that is when my curiosity kicked in.

Within a couple of hours I felt sick – extremely sick. I vomited, lost my bearings and was 'out of sorts' for hours and in that moment, eating those brownies was something I did not want to indulge in again.

As it turned out, a few weeks later I caved in and thought I would give the brownies another go. To my surprise I didn't have the same

Unbosoming

reaction as the first time although I can't say I loved the experience of how it made me feel. I decided it wasn't for me anymore.

Each week we gathered and had lots of parties. Although there was a lot happening around me that I witnessed, I personally didn't get involved in experimenting with the party drugs that Annabelle and crew were revelling in. I was happy smoking a 'scoob' and enjoyed a few drinks. That was enough for me. What I did do, was to learn a lesson.

I always felt safe in the surroundings when I was with Annabelle, but as time went on the scenarios got a little messier. I felt like I was putting myself in compromising positions that started to make me feel uncomfortable. The gatherings got bigger, the crowd became unruly and the amount of alcohol and drugs that were being consumed were extreme.

My turning point was one Saturday evening when I found myself in a dangerous situation.

A man whom I had only known for a short time caught me off guard and informally began to grope me. As I tried to push him away, he became aggressive and was 'man handling' me in an inappropriate manner. Thankfully having my wits about me and with quick thinking, I managed to free myself from the situation. It was that exact night I knew it was time for me to get out!

I left Annabelle's that evening and knew the friendship and the weekly parties weren't serving me a purpose anymore. Her and I never had a falling out. I just decided it was time for me to move on.

Back in 2009 was the last time I provided a salon service for Annabelle. It was also the last time I saw her. To this day I am still owed $165. Annabelle did a runner! The IOU (I owe you) that I always happily agreed to never got paid back. Honestly, I never imagined that Annabelle would skip town and do that to me!

Everything that I witnessed throughout the times we had together were some of the most invaluable life lessons ever! I became mentally stronger about the choices I was making and knew that I didn't have to take part in what others were doing to fit in.

At times we need to reflect on ourselves, be true to who we are and what we believe and have the courage to 'stand our ground'.

CHASING THE DOLLARS

My gorgeous client Sassy wanted to stop gambling, but for whatever reason it continued to play a big part in her life.

Her friend Tarni, also a client of mine, would receive desperate calls for help and on many occasions had to drop everything to bail Sassy out by giving her money to cover her tracks.

From what I had been told, all the desperate and erratic cries of help from Sassy were making Tarni feel concerned about how to support her. I think Tarni felt sorry for Sassy and wanted to keep her secret safe. I did not blame her, but I could see how this situation was weighing Tarni down.

When Sassy came into the salon her presence was always genuinely beautiful and I really enjoyed our time together. We chatted a lot and had always openly discussed her gambling addiction. I listened to what Sassy told me and felt as though there was a sudden urge for her to win money so that she could maintain her independence whilst also sustaining her smoking and drinking habit. Sassy agreed!

After many discussions and years gone by both Tarni and I came to realise that Sassy had an inability to keep things in perspective, which clearly contributed to the ongoing gambling and losses that impacted her life. In many ways it made her desperate. Although there were times that Sassy had a win, the losses were greater, yet it didn't stop her from repeatedly betting and losing more and more money.

Tarni backed away from Sassy for a while and focused on herself and her family which in turn made Sassy realise how much she missed having Tarni in her life.

It took some time but eventually Sassy paid Tarni all the money that she owed her. Sassy came to realise that seeking help for her addiction was what saved her and I am so glad it did! I am pleased to say that she is now on a better life path for herself which is a real credit to her.

Just like Sassy, Eric is another client I have known for about 15 years who also became a compulsive gambler and lost over $35,000 in less than six months. When Eric's marriage broke down, it led him down a path of self-destruction.

Eric was the first to admit he "fu**ed up big time" and acknowledged that he had a problem! We spoke about his addiction and how it made him feel and Eric told me he was going to make it a priority to focus on strategies that would break his gambling habit. Thankfully Eric tackled his issue head on and sourced out the help that he needed.

Eric said that gambling had robbed him of his energy and happiness and that he realised he wanted to reclaim his life.

As time went on, I witnessed Eric's transformation and was inspired by the way he got himself back into a positive mindset.

I was extremely happy when I first met with Roxy who was a woman whom Eric got to know at a Gamblers Anonymous meeting. Watching both Eric and Roxy support one another in those small moments that I witnessed at the salon, gave me hope that you can make changes for the better if you are willing to work at it.

As months went by they fell in love and within a few years went on to have two children, Ally and Coby. In 2012 they packed up their little family and moved interstate to start their next chapter in life together.

Identify and understand what you want to improve or change and find a big enough desire to do it. Remember there are no short cuts in this life; work hard towards your personal goals and you will be rewarded. It may take time, but it is possible!

CHALICE WINE

Father Hollis was an alcoholic and I often wondered how he stood up at church from week to week preaching to the congregation.

Hollis became a topic of conversation within the community because he was consuming alcohol, lots of it and for many years everyone would often talk about Hollis's drinking habits. People would laugh and joke about him behind his back and his alcoholism went unaddressed for many years, although it didn't go unnoticed!

Unbosoming

I wonder if Father Hollis stole money from the church collection to fund his boozy ways?

I was quite young, yet old enough to understand and I will never forget what Hollis looked like. I am sure there were times when he hadn't showered for days. His personal hygiene needed attention and it was obvious. I remember him always looking so greasy and oily and he would spit when he spoke. He was yuck! I also thought Hollis was creepy to be around. I would often just stare at him from a distance when I was in church so I could watch his body language. He would appear disoriented and confused and a little baffling in his communication. At the time I thought it was funny. I questioned how he would maintain composure after a few bevvies.

I was about 15 years old when I decided that I would back away from going to church every Sunday with Mum. Quite simply I didn't enjoy it anymore.

It's important to allow our children to make some active decisions for themselves at certain times in their lives and I am grateful that after a while, my mum gave up on asking me to go with her.

As I got older and I understood more, I went on to choose the moments or occasions that resonated with me when re-entering a church. I have no regrets in not following the Catholic faith the same way as I once did, but I still have faith, a lot of it!

For whatever reason at the age of 16 I came across a little book about Buddhism and I am so happy that I did.

My own belief system is filled with everything I have learnt and continue to learn. I base my faith on my experiences, my reality and whatever is going on around me.

This is what I notice the most.

CHOCOLATE BOX

At the salon we all love Dane. He is a great man who is down to earth, a bit of a risk-taker, up front in his communication and has an incredible smile. One of my team members has always told me that she really enjoys the conversations that she has with Dane and loves being in his presence. I would have to agree! Dane really is a top bloke!

My team member has been Dane's hairdresser for more than 12 years and is the 'go-to person' when he books in for a haircut.

A week prior to Melbourne's lockdown in 2020, Dane gifted us with marijuana infused chocolate treats. They are the sort of treats that I have not eaten for quite some time and so when I got home that day, I just tucked them away in the fridge not giving them a second thought.

When the moment was right and in my own personal time, after being locked away at home for nearly 100 days and with only the freedom for a little exercise, the curiosity of a treat got the better of me. It was a sunny afternoon when I decided to indulge in eating one of the chocolates. A taste test with a difference. I then went on a leisurely walk and it turned out to be a walk with a difference. It felt like I was walking slowly as though I was getting nowhere fast and my body felt heavy like it was sinking to the ground. I was laughing to myself. It was so entertaining!

When you look at these little chocolate treats you would not know any different. They look like a chocolate you would pick right out of a candy box!

For me personally, anything in moderation is the key when I try something. My choice!

Thank you Dane.

Life really is like a box of chocolates!

It's okay to be curious but remember to be moderate and safe.

CLOSET BEVVY

Out of the blue one day Jerry says to me, "I'm an alcoholic, I think I'm a closet drinker, can you tell? I always drink before I arrive to my appointment."

It is fair to say that I have had many clients who have shared this very conversation with me and many of them are such wonderful people. For different reasons they feel as though they need to regularly drink alcohol. Many have said to me that alcohol keeps them going and underlying what others may see on the surface, they have had experiences in their lives that have affected them mentally, physically and emotionally. Alcohol is their survival tool. It allows them to forget what they don't want to think about and helps to shut out what is on their mind.

This is certainly not the reason why all alcoholics drink. Others have told me they just love to have a drink and simply enjoy it. At times they have way too many without even realising it and yet, will keep drinking!

My gorgeous salon client Jerry would often drink alcohol at home when no one was around and then would refill the bottle with a liquid that looked similar in colour to the alcohol he had consumed. When Jerry was confronted by his husband Byron about the mysterious liquid in the bottle, he would always act as though he was innocent to the fact! The worst part of Jerry's excessive drinking was that he openly told me that he became aggressive, rude and disrespectful towards Byron when he had too much to drink.

One day Jerry was being recorded whilst refilling an empty alcohol bottle and apparently Byron took the liberty to address Jerry in action by showing him the evidence.

That is when things took a turning point. Byron decided to tell his older sister what was going on. As a family they started to talk through what was happening in their home and how to best deal with Jerry's 'closet drinking' habits. For a little while Jerry made small improvements and wasn't drinking as much as usual but it wasn't long before his old habits kicked in. To this day he is still drinking alcohol and lots of it.

Jerry is not hiding his reality anymore. Byron does not like being in his presence and they have gone their separate ways.

I know this story may resonate with people as it is a common problem in many homes.
It is difficult at times for everyone involved and can put family members in compromising and dangerous situations. Unfortunately, you just don't know how to help that person you love and care about when they don't make the decision to help themselves.

There is support out there for people when they are wanting to make changes in their life.

I have witnessed positive outcomes and have been inspired by others who have worked hard to improve their individual circumstances.

The key is to be committed and ready to transition into the next best version of yourself!

FEATHER LANDING

If you know Jace today, as the grounded and mature adult he is, you wouldn't imagine that growing up, his life was unstable and at times, dysfunctional.

It is fair to say that Jace experienced lots of good times with his family and friends and was blessed with influential and positive role models, especially his nonno, who is now a flying angel in heaven.

Despite being a witness to his mother's many different behavioural patterns over the years, associated to mental health, Jace utilised his experiences and learnings to help people in need. His line of work contributes to supporting those in vulnerable situations and it is a true testament to Jace that he willingly turned his own life around to be of benefit to himself and others.

He is now aged 29 and is a father. He and his gorgeous wife Tay have two beautiful sons and they are personal friends of mine. They are all a pleasure to be around.

As a young adult, an unexpected turn of events saw him flee Australia to travel to Malta. His mission was to find a missing person – his own mother! It is fair to say he needed a lot of luck and hope on his side. This is exactly what happened to this young couple when they were in their early 20s.

Jace and Taye were on a mission like no other. The end in sight seemed gloomy and alarming. In their mind they had no idea where to start or what road to travel. The chances of finding a missing person in a country they were not familiar with was very slim. Furthermore, the language barrier made this situation even more challenging!

Jace understood his mum, Angelica, had been dealing with mental health issues for quite some time. Over the years, growing up in the family home became difficult for Jace. As a young person, watching a loved one struggle with mental health can make you feel lost and alone and you are not sure what you can do to help.

No one ever imagined that Angelica was capable of vanishing and just like that in a fleeting moment it happened! She was gone! Her erratic and unexpected disappearance was extremely overwhelming and scary to say the least.

Jace and Taye made their way from Australia to Malta and then to Italy all within a few days. They would ask a million questions to any relatives and family members who last saw Angelica and, with not much to go on, their own anxiety and stress levels began to take a toll on their own health.

Trying to stay calm and positive was not an easy task for Jace or Taye. They were both feeling a million different emotions and in their minds were visualising many different scenarios that would make them feel constantly frightened. Would they ever find Angelica? Was she alive? Did someone kidnap her? Was she even in Italy? Or was she in Malta? This was the million dollar question.

It took many embassies and police work before she was finally located! Angelica was in a psychiatric hospital in Sicily in Italy. The struggle now was for Jace and Taye to get her discharged from this 'asylum' looking place and bring her home. She was incoherent and had no belongings with her, not even a passport.

Taking a break to fuel their body with coffee and food was the best move at the right moment in a little cafe in Sicily. As they were sitting outside on a very beautiful day with blue skies and the sun shining, it was in this one given moment that Taye looked up and noticed a white feather gently making its way down from the sky towards her. As she watched it gracefully flow through the air, thoughts of her abuelo (Spanish for grandpa) filled her heart and mind with warmth and positivity. Taye experienced a glimmer of hope that Angelica would be brought home safely. The thought of accomplishing the impossible seemed more realistic than ever. And just like that, the beautiful white feather landed perfectly right on Taye's foot. Her angel abuelo had made his presence felt and at that special moment Jace and Taye began a new journey which took a turning point for the better.

Mental health is affecting people in our society all over the world. For many it can have detrimental outcomes and can show clear characteristics that vary depending on the severity of the condition. Reach out and seek immediate assistance if you think a friend or family member is an any danger. Sometimes the carers need support too.

UNITED FOR GLOBAL MENTAL HEALTH
Unitedgmh.org

Mental Health and Addiction

LIFESTYLE OF COCAINE

Believe it or not 'Cocaine Living' is a thing! There are a lot of people dependent on this party drug for many different reasons. They often say cocaine is for rich people. I would confirm that it is not. It is being consumed by many and it is a lot closer to you than you think.

I am a person who has communicated very openly with my own kids about many things that perhaps other parents would not agree with. I have no hesitation in 'keeping it real' when having discussions about drugs and their effects.

I have lived in Craigieburn since the age of five, grew up in the community and have worked in the salon for over 30 years. When I say I have heard a lot, seen a lot and experienced a lot, believe me I have!

Ashlyn, who was employed by a multi-million-dollar company, was living the life, so she told me.
"I've been snorting cocaine for over 10 years now with my boss and the people we work with would not have a clue."

Over time Ashlyn worked her way up the corporate ladder and with a yearly salary of over $300,000 she was able to live a flamboyant life. Whenever I did her hair, I was always interested and intrigued by the conversation. Ashlyn's life was like watching a Hollywood movie. Buying clothes, shoes, accessories, cars, a penthouse and living like a rich girl was all Ashlyn knew. One thing was that her dress code was always top of the range. Immaculately groomed from top to toe, her fashion was very impressive!

Although the money was in abundance, the heart seemed very empty. Love was not in Ashlyn's favour and relationships always seemed to crumble. I believe Ashlyn continued to indulge in drugs to mask her underlying sadness and pain. As much as I thought that she was a beautiful person, I felt sorry for her. After many discussions it was made clear to me that her childhood played a big part in the person she grew up to become.

When it comes to party drugs and ongoing substance abuse, as a parent, I don't hesitate to speak up. Brooke and Corey are my children and I have always made it very clear that they can come to me and discuss anything. I have no regrets about our very open and liberating chats! Our home has always been a space for family and friends to enjoy. And just like the chats I have with my own kids, I am always available to support and listen to others.

I have seen many young vulnerable teens turn to drugs. It does happen and can happen to any person, young or old.

Don't be afraid to talk about topics associated to drugs.
Create an awareness about the impact it can have on one's life.
The reality is, drugs are becoming an epidemic and it's frightening.

Be aware of the choices you make.

LOST BOY

Getting caught up in a lifestyle of selling drugs is something Damon had been doing for years. He told me he was only 12 years old when drugs were first introduced to him. At 19 years of age, when I last saw Damon, he looked scattered and withdrawn. His skin was full of sores and his teeth looked rotten and discoloured. He was so thin and fragile and seemed to have aged 20 years. In all honesty, Damon looked so much older than his 19-year-old self.

His mum Chrystella was in her mid 60s and didn't speak much English. Damon was an only child who rarely attended school. When I would see him at the local shop near the salon I would always ask, "Why aren't you at school?" and he would just giggle and then take off on his push bike. It was as though he knew he was being a naughty kid wagging school, but I don't think his mum would have known any different. When I saw Damon and Chrystella together, I got the impression that the man of the house was Damon. He would always speak for her.

To Damon's credit, at every salon visit he always had lovely manners and was gently spoken. He did not have any other family other than his mum. As I got to know Damon better, I began to understand many of his underlying issues.

Life was not so kind to Damon and his mum. Chrystella told me her husband Fernando was a bully and an alcoholic and passed away in the early '90s when Damon was only nine years old. Both Damon and Chrystella had been victims to the abuse and were mentally scarred and traumatised. After Fernando passed away Chrystella was left alone, isolated and abandoned at home. Living in a community and not having friends or family was one of the many challenges she faced. Not being able to speak the English language very well was the biggest barrier of all. Chrystella was lovely. A very gentle woman who always seemed withdrawn and afraid. You would always sense a level of shyness and fragility about her.

As the years went on Damon was dealing drugs, sourcing them out, delivering them, chasing money and at times being chased himself. This became a way of life for Damon.

Chrystella loved her son so much. You could see the love in her eyes every time she would smile at him. I am not sure that she knew what to do with a young, energetic, 12-year-old boy who was finding his way in a new community. Damon was young and naïve. Over time he became misled and influenced by people who took advantage of his innocence.

Having migrated to Australia, being in a foreign country and not being able to speak the language fluently was a huge barrier for both Damon and Chrystella.

I will always remember Damon as a vulnerable, sweet and mischievous 12-year-old boy. Damon passed away just before his 20th birthday.

The choices we make each day play a big part in determining our fate.

Sometimes we need to further know the stories, backgrounds and lifestyles of others to better understand them.

MIND MATTERS AND PRESCRIPTION DRUGS

The power of the mind works in mysterious ways!

I knew Foxy gambled the family savings away. It would be only a matter of time before things escalated and got worse for him. With a gambling addiction comes a sense of desperation. When Foxy lost his job due to stealing, I knew that was his biggest blow! He had already lost everything else around him including his wife and family and the house was next.

Mental Health and Addiction

I didn't know until months later that Foxy also became addicted to prescription drugs. Foxy's ex-wife Lola told me he had been abusing the drugs by consuming more than the prescribed amount. She was concerned for him. His pattern of behaviour made him always seem spaced out and unaware of what was happening around him.

On this one day at the salon I noticed a dramatic change in the way Foxy spoke to me and it seemed unusual, a little aggressive. Being in his presence suddenly felt uneasy, even scary. His behaviour was erratic and listening to him was not very pleasant. I remained calm as I always do when confronted with circumstances that feel a little dangerous. Nevertheless, I continued to cut his hair.

I knew that if I went along with the flow of his rambled conversation and agreed with what was being said, hopefully I would be okay. For me being alert and practising the art of listening twice and talking once allows time to assess a situation before responding.

Just before completing a dry off, he became weird. He snapped at me when I asked about applying product in his hair. Out of nowhere he got up, made his way to the reception desk, paid for the service and then turned around and left. It was as though in that very moment he became a different person.

What had just happened? I couldn't even explain it!

Foxy and Lola are now divorced and no longer live in my community. I am happy that Lola is safe and not in danger any longer. The last time I saw her she was wearing sunglasses and when she held them down to make eye contact with me, her black and bruised eye told a story in itself!

Overuse of prescription drugs can become very problematic. Early intervention may prevent the problem from turning into an addiction. Keep an eye out for your loved ones and seek help if you suspect a situation may get out of control.

MONEY FOR MEDICATION

Prescription drugs prescribed for people who need medication is one thing, but when these drugs are used to make money then that is another. When Johnson confessed his pill moneymaking scheme to me, I wasn't surprised. On the contrary, I was very concerned.

Johnson was dependant on his daily medication to function in a safe manner and the thought of him selling what he personally needed for his own mind and body, set off alarm bells for me. His erratic and aggressive behaviour was very obvious, and his mum Kiely often struggled with trying to calm him down.

Johnson has always been quite the introvert and constantly displayed traits of aggression. He became continually distracted and was always fidgety. I have known Johnson and his family since 1999 and in his primary school years Johnson was diagnosed with ADHD. As he got older I continued to witness that Johnson was deteriorating on many levels.

I believe it is important to share your feelings, thoughts and experiences with others to release the build-up in our minds that can often lead to other setbacks. This is exactly what Kiely did each time we crossed paths. Whether it was at the salon or out in the community, Kiely was always ready to vent her thoughts.

She often struggled with trying to settle him down and watching her feel helpless and frustrated was an ongoing and constant reminder that Johnson was not coping with this very common medical condition that so many others are facing daily. Listening to a mother who in many ways suffers in silence whilst trying to find every possible way to help her child is heart-breaking.

Over time I have learnt so much about Johnson and Kiely. Their personal life journey has entailed way too much for way too long. Aside from Johnson's medical condition, this family has faced hardship and struggles that you would not wish upon anyone.

When I was cutting Johnson's hair one day he told me about his $60 pill-popping adventure that earns him quick and easy money and on that same day I felt compelled to let Kiely know about the conversation that Johnson had just shared with me.

To be honest I often felt a little afraid when I was in his presence. I never knew what to expect and when Johnson would have constant and sudden outbursts, it made me feel afraid of what may happen. It was even more challenging for Kiely who had to deal with Johnson and his unexpected, dangerous behaviours.

Johnson was a walking time bomb, and his behaviour and neglect of medication became a recipe for disaster. Sadly, he was making the choice to sell his much-needed medication, rather than ingesting it for himself.

I have not seen Kiely or Johnson for more than three years now and I am not sure what happened to them. All I do know is that what I witnessed on many occasions was not pleasant.

My hope is that Johnson his taking his prescribed medication and has stopped selling pills to other young members of the community.

NANNA, 'Tee' and DADDY

When I first held this precious little baby, I never imagined her young life would spin around in circles the way it did! Tee's early childhood years seemed to be a little like taking a ride on a roller coaster. From one day to another her journey moved in many different directions. Yet despite the twists and turns, one thing remained and that was Tee's glowing inner spark!

To the credit of Nanna – who loves Tee so much – and a determined daddy – a reformed drug addict – in time Tee would be well on her way to wonderful new beginnings.

More than a decade ago I was lucky to have crossed paths with Nanna and over such a long period of time I have learnt so much from her. I am grateful for all the moments we have spent together and look forward to many more. I admire Nanna and see her as a person who works extremely hard to support her loved ones. One trait I just adore about Nanna is her laughter. It is loud and so infectious; you can't help but feel an abundance of energy when you are around her. To top it off, she has a gorgeous smile that is always welcoming.

This gem of a woman will do the best she can to help her family. Whether it be cooking, cleaning, trying out a new business venture, rescuing an animal (literally any animal), or running her family around to get things done, Nanna is a kind-hearted person and so much more. She is a beautiful soul who wears her heart on her sleeve and I have always loved being in her presence. Nanna, you are an amazing woman, don't ever forget that!

When I see Nanna and Tee together, I can feel the precious and loving bond that they share, and it is very special and unique. Tee definitely has Nanna's zest for life and flaunts a warmth that you cannot help but fall in love with. I feel blessed to have been able to watch this dazzling little girl grow over the years and have always embraced the joy and happiness that her free spirit radiates. Do not ever lose that glow about you, Tee.

In May 2021 Tee celebrated her eighth birthday and together with Nanna and Daddy we had such an awesome time on our holiday. It was extra special this year and I especially enjoyed our beach walks and the conversations that Tee and I shared. You are such a bright and intelligent young lady and much older than your years!

Wow, how time flies; it doesn't seem that long ago that I was giving Tee baby cuddles. I miss you Tee.

This story is not complete without giving credit to Daddy, who in time found the willpower and inner strength to diverge from a life path he was once leading. Although Daddy endured many setbacks and failures due to his addiction and drug abuse, the life choices that he made, and his personal development over recent years have been astounding. He was able to make a decision to move from the pathway of self-destruction and darkness to one of responsibility, growth and hope.

Watching Daddy progress and develop over the years made me realise that change can happen when 'YOU' make a commitment to a better life for yourself and your loved ones. I believe that it was Tee who gave Daddy a greater sense of purpose and alignment. Having a daughter that Daddy loved so much and working on strategies to be her mentor and role model would eventually become his focus. Daddy is proof that anything can happen when you set goals and work towards achieving them!

Daddy is a success story in himself!

Despite everything they have all been though, I can honestly say this daddy has grown into a grounded and influential father figure who has taken his beloved daughter Tee under his wing, and together they are blossoming.

I am so happy that Daddy and Tee are enjoying their life together as a family in their new home. Daddy, you should be so proud of all your accomplishments!

The ongoing support I witnessed Nanna display through many of the ups and downs is a true testament that her love, determination and ongoing vision of hope can be a saviour for others in need. With the love that Nanna and Daddy have for Tee, may the future sparkle even brighter. Celebrate life and continue making memories together.

Thank you Daddy for choosing me to be Tee's godmother. I am truly honoured. I am so grateful you have allowed me in some way to be a part of this journey with you all.

I hope that in sharing this short story with others you may come to realise that just like Nanna, Tee and Daddy, it is possible to look forward to better days when you don't give up.

I have so much love for Nanna, Tee and Daddy XXX.

Mental Health and Addiction

"Character cannot be developed in ease and quiet. Only through experience of trial and suffering can the soul be strengthened, ambition inspired, and success achieved."
Helen Keller

PILL PRESSURE

At the age of 15 McKinley started taking diet pills, amongst other pills and ended up in hospital on several occasions. She had an adverse reaction to the pills she had been consuming and at one stage remained in hospital for days.

Janaki is McKinley's mum, and we have known one another for about three years. When Janaki first told me about the container of medications she found in her daughter's bedroom, she was horrified. She didn't understand what was going on and when she confronted her daughter about it, McKinley was outraged! From what I remember Janaki telling me, they had a massive fight and McKinley took off and did not come home for a few days.

So much has happened in the last few years and just like other parents and carers of young people, Janaki feels as though she just doesn't know how to help her daughter.

I often hear stories like this one and remember growing up with friends who also took diet pills as a way of losing weight. The pressure of looking a certain way is becoming more apparent and body image issues are affecting many people, more than we can imagine.

Now at the age of 17, McKinley has a long journey ahead of her. Becoming the person McKinley wants to be will be very much determined by the choices and decisions that she will make. Right now, all McKinley can see is negativity and a dark hole. Her self-doubt is consuming her, and she seeks comfort in food to combat her sadness or alternately will not eat at all. What I see is a real beauty about McKinley that glows, but just like many other teenagers her low self-esteem and insecurities are making her feel unworthy and unattractive and it is as though everything and everyone annoys her.

Rather than focusing on being happy within herself and learning to love and accept who she is, all I hear is negative talk. "I don't want to do that, I can't do that, I am not good at doing that. I am so overweight. I hate looking at myself in the mirror." So much negative self-talk consumes her.

There is so much goodness about McKinley that she has not discovered about herself. This negativity will only carry her deeper into a way of life that will ultimately continue to hold her back. I don't want her to be unhappy, sad, and lonely anymore.

When I look at McKinley, I do see that she can transition into an inspiring young adult who can be self-driven and caring. I have always seen these qualities in her. I just hope that McKinley finds that inner spark within herself and begins to accept and recognise that she is a special and valued person.

When we start to appreciate the good things around us and begin to love being who we are, it can make a significant impact on how we can feel. There can always be a turning point in a happier direction. You, yourself need to be in the driving seat, stay in your own laneway and keep going for YOU! When we start to determine the outcome or resolution that we are hoping for, things in our lives can change for the better.

Insecurity is a real trap and what people don't always recognise is that we can hurt ourselves the most. There are people around you who are wanting to see you happy, to smile and to embrace and enjoy being you.

The key is to find all that goodness in yourself and so much more.

PRESCRIPTION MEDICATION

I had always known Dora to be a gorgeous girl with the most beautiful eyes and a flair for fashion. I loved her style and would always compliment her eye make-up, the funky clothing she wore or her bright smile. Dora was always polite and lovely to talk to. I was given an opportunity to get to know her at the age of 14 when she took part in the Body Culture Grow-Learn-Develop Program, also known as 'Wheelz in Motion'.

Violetta was Dora's mum, and we have known one another for more than 20 years. We met at the salon and over time we became friends. I often saw her out in the community as we were both involved in the local football club. We chatted on many occasions and on one particular day, Violetta told me about Dora's sudden health condition and the problems that she was experiencing. I felt really overwhelmed with what I was hearing. I knew a little about asthma, as my son also experienced health issues with this condition when he was eight years old. He ended up in hospital but thankfully over time he got better and now manages his asthma quite well.

Six months prior to Dora celebrating her 18th birthday she was diagnosed with chronic asthma. Violetta and her family watched Dora change in many ways. A once bubbly teenager was now a young 18-year-old who closed herself off from the outside world. It was a life-changing experience for everyone in the family, especially Dora. Each day Violetta watched on as her daughter began to struggle mentally, emotionally and physically.

One day, out of the blue, Violetta called me at work and asked if I would be able to pop into her home to see her. I could hear in her voice that she was struggling to communicate. Suddenly she broke down and began crying uncontrollably. We arranged a time and later that day I called in to see her. I was really worried about what was going on and when I arrived Violetta looked deflated and fragile. As I entered the house I saw Dora lying down on the couch. All I saw in that very moment was a tired and sad young girl who seemed down and out on herself. I had never seen her like this before.

Violetta asked me to take a seat and proceeded to make us all a hot drink. Whilst she was doing that I began chatting with Dora. We started talking and our conversation flowed naturally. I kept asking open-ended questions in the hope that I would get a reply. To my surprise, she opened up and we continued to chat.

As time went on Dora slowly sat up in the couch and started drinking some water. I could sense just a glimmer of hope within her. The lovely smile that I normally saw was what I was witnessing in this moment and it was nice.

As we continued to chat I began to understand that as a result of Dora taking steroids to manage her asthma, her appetite increased dramatically, and this made her gain weight – a lot of weight.

We continued to communicate about a variety of topics and then tapped into some of the memories that Dora had experienced when she took part in the Body Culture program. I asked Dora if she still had the student training manual and I was pleased that she had kept it. I asked if she was able to get it so that we could revisit some of the topics that were of interest to her. When Dora started looking over the content in the training manual, she made a comment that the quotes made her feel more positive about herself. We discussed each quote one by one, and I asked Dora what message came to mind when reading the individual quotes and what it meant to her. It was nice to just sit and listen and allow Dora to share her thoughts. We decided to print out the positive quotes and place them up around Dora's bedroom, as a reminder to take time each day to reflect on these. They could help with empowering herself.

I knew that there was a long way to go before Dora would bounce back to loving herself. I hoped that in time she would regain some inner strength and self-belief that would help to bring out the best version of her! The wonderful qualities about this young woman are in abundance! A couple of hours had passed by, and I was filled with a little more hope that Dora would make time to work on strategies to improve her current situation.

Ultimately managing any health issue can be challenging and over time it gets tiring and stressful. If we can find it in ourselves to manage what we are dealing with as best we can, whilst also focusing on some of the positive things in our lives that make us happy, then we have hope.

Violetta and I also spoke to Dora about visiting her local GP. We discussed that she would be able to express her concerns in confidence and that getting a mental health plan to see a psychologist would provide some extra support.

At times and for many of us, it can be a very challenging process to maintain an ideal weight. I often wonder, "What is an ideal weight?"

Discussing weight, body size and shape has become a common conversation that can really affect people. For those people who are experiencing health issues and need to take prescription medication that unwillingly makes them put on weight, it is a struggle. Clearly, for many, it can be an ongoing problem in more ways than one. Maintaining healthy eating habits and exercising regularly doesn't always have the outcome that people are looking for.

In this world there are so many people who are battling all kinds of issues with their weight, body size and shape. Over the past three decades in my salon workplace, I have spoken with many people who suffer body image concerns and a lot of it has nothing to do with prescribed medication. Technology, social media and the amount of time spent on devices, whether it be mobile phone, iPads or laptop, is a worry for many reasons and has a lot to answer for! That is a whole other topic in itself!

It took three years of commitment and lots of self-motivation to see Dora's health progress for the better. Day by day, one step at a time, improvements were being made. Dora had a confidence about her that I always knew she had within her. Each time we spoke I was truly inspired by the positive changes that she was making. It had nothing to do with her weight but everything to do with her being happier within herself.

The beautiful support from Dora's family and friends was imperative to her recovery. Her state of mind is a lot more positive and today all I see is a person who, in time, accepted and acknowledged her health condition and sourced out ways to look after herself.

Mental Health and Addiction

Dora is now 29 years old, has a six-year-old daughter and is married to a wonderful person. They live in NSW on a little hobby farm and Dora works at the local community centre as a youth mentor. I am so proud of her.

Violetta lost her husband about 12 months ago and recently moved to be closer to Dora and her family.

Dora you are a true gem!

It is important to have a voice.
Get the support you need.
You don't have to become an ongoing victim.

You are important and you are worthy of being in safe and healthy spaces.

> "Success is liking yourself, liking what you do, and liking how you do it."
> **Maya Angelou**

SUDDENLY

My beautiful client Patsy is a gentle soul, and it came as a real shock to me when I found out her son Amish suddenly passed. I was devastated.

I will always remember the look on Patsy's face when I saw her the first time after the accident. Her smile appeared to be forced. You could feel the distress, pain and sadness that was so heavy on her heart. None of us can ever imagine what is going on in someone's mind just before they take their own life.

Amish was young, handsome and always well-groomed. When he came into the salon for haircuts, I always liked our conversations. He was well spoken, mature for a 17-year-old and I thought he was quite intelligent. I recall Patsy always telling me that she wished he had friends and could not understand why he did not get out and socialise much.

Just like Amish, who passed away more than 20 years ago, there are many others who don't cope well with life and living in our society. For many, getting out of the house is a struggle.

For Patsy it has been a long journey moving forward with so many unanswered questions that she will never get an answer to. It has been more than two decades since her son passed away and she is still withdrawn and isolated from society. Patsy lives alone and does not go out much anymore. Her daily routine bounds her to her home which is her choice, and she smokes and drinks alcohol excessively. Her health has deteriorated, and Patsy is now battling with her own mental health issues and has stage three breast cancer.

When a loved one takes their own life, the family are left here with the reality of this situation, and the next chapter, which involves finding a way to get through this, begins to unfold. They say that 'time heals everything', and in many ways I agree. Yet, for many healing a broken heart, the loss of a loved one, especially a child, is irreparable. This I also agree with!

One of the most common conversations in the salon these days is with parents who express that they find it difficult to communicate with their kids. So many of the parents I speak with talk about how their kids stay in their bedrooms all day and hardly connect with the family. Furthermore, the kids do not even make an appearance at mealtimes and their personal hygiene is also being overlooked. Parents are struggling and children are isolating themselves away from others.

In so many homes the issues that a family member may be facing go unnoticed, unintentionally. Each person is battling with their own thoughts and the issues they are dealing with will vary depending on their circumstances. Appreciate your loved ones because they can be here today and gone tomorrow.

Embrace the power of connecting with others.

TAKE A PUNT

"I just put a $100,000 bet on a horse to win and I lost. It came in 2nd!"

Kippa, who I have known for a long time, is always betting on the horses or the dogs. He is a big punter, and he makes big dollar bets!

Kippa has the funds to back his spending and is a very successful businessman. The company he owns is worth millions and he is always flying around the world living the life. So he says.

I really like Kippa. He is a great guy, very approachable, funny and somewhat charming. Every time I would cut his hair, he would talk about his adventures, who he has met and what he may be buying next. To be honest I do not say too much at all. Kippa is like an open book, always eager to share his stories and I am the sounding board, listening. I find Kippa interesting and always look forward to seeing him.

Kippa is happy, always smiling and has a positive vibe whenever he comes to the salon. He reminds me of a rock star for some reason. His presence is captivating. I love that he pumps lots of money into charity organisations and shares his wealth with his dearest and nearest. His family are beautiful, they are genuinely lovely people, and I am so glad that in my early 20s, I got to meet him.

Kippa would always bet big, tip me generously, and never hesitated in disclosing that he has been gambling excessively for more than two decades!

UNKNOWN TERRORTORY

I met with Christos and Flora over 30 years ago. They are parents to an only child and her name is Rhea. I adored this family. They were salon clients back in the late '80s and I had a lot of respect for them. They were beautiful people, a very lovely family.

As the years went on Christos and Flora witnessed their daughter become an aggressive and bitter teenager who over time turned into an enraged and bitter young woman. Rhea's parents found this change in her to be very confronting and had no idea what was wrong with their daughter.

The truth is, Christos and Flora were completely unaware about illegal drugs and substance abuse. They would have never imagined that their daughter was dabbling with drugs and getting caught up in this way of life.

I would listen to what Rhea's parents would tell me and was aware they had no idea about Rhea's secret lifestyle. The situation that Rhea had put herself in was dangerous and destructive!

I found myself being challenged at times and had so many conflicting thoughts going on in my head. I knew what Rhea was doing to herself and I also knew who Rhea was associated with. I needed to suppress all that information because I had already been hit up by a certain someone who warned me about keeping my mouth shut, not only about Rhea but many other things that I was aware of! I learnt quickly that knowing everything was making out that I knew fu** all.

Nate was Rhea's other half. I wouldn't say boyfriend, he was like a fu**ed up fake friend with benefits. Fu**ed up is an understatement! Nate was more like a controlling, manipulative cu*t of a person who used people to benefit himself!

Rhea puts out and provides sex to Nate and Nate supplies the drugs to Rhea. More sex, more drugs!

Rhea was so consumed with her ongoing substance abuse. Over time she continued taking a cocktail of illegal drugs and this clearly made her perception about everything distorted. She seemed disoriented and emotionally bitter about everyone and everything.

To this day I clearly remember Rhea and her parents being in the salon. Christos and Flora had an underlying agenda to meet with Rhea and had asked for my support. They had not seen her for more than a year and I had not seen Rhea for well over three years. They thought I would be able to get through to Rhea and find out what was going on with her. The truth is I knew more

Unbosoming

than I wanted to know and having Rhea back in the salon made me feel uneasy.

Despite everything I was feeling, I could not overlook the sadness on Christos and Flora's faces. They had agreed to pay for Rhea's hair colour and pampering session at the salon and in return Rhea agreed to spend time with her parents after the salon service.

Not long after Rhea arrived at the salon, her parents popped in to see her. When they saw their daughter, they got a shock and Flora broke down in tears. I was trying to concentrate on my work but was so distracted. The situation made me feel a little anxious.

I finished applying Rhea's colour and made her a coffee. She went out the back to have a smoke and while she was out of sight, I subtly asked Christos and Flora to join me outside at the front of salon, so that we could have a quick chat.

"Christos, Flora, I am so sorry to tell you this, but your daughter Rhea is under the influence of drugs."

Instantly I felt their heartache! The confusion set in. They looked at one another with disbelief and I could see the darkness and depth in their sad and tired eyes. They were hurting. They wanted to understand. They were lost for words.

I never saw Rhea, Christos or Flora after that day. It was as though they had all disappeared!

Christos and Flora just wanted great things to happen for Rhea. Sadly, that was not to be.

Mental Health and Addiction

In late 2012 Rhea overdosed and took her own life, aged 23.

Until you are confronted with being around someone who has a drug addiction you really cannot imagine how it impacts everyone around them.

Drugs are an epidemic in our society today, more so than ever.
Millions of people have lost loved ones to substance abuse.
We have one life and one chance and many people who care about us.
To see a life lost to a ruthless drug is sad.
Everyone can subject themselves to loss of life by experimenting with drugs.
Can you imagine life ending because of a drug?

Unfortunately for so many families it has become a reality.

REMEMBER – Peer pressure may lead to negative or dangerous circumstances.

If you are not happy to do something, have the strength to say NO!

VB CANS X 6

Kade remembers the motel room as though he was there not too long ago. One day, he came out and said to me, "When I was a young boy my parents would always leave me alone in a dark motel room with the TV blaring. They would hand me a 6-pack of VB cans, a packet of potato chips and then turn around and leave, shutting the door behind them. All I remember is waking up in a head fog the next morning. This went on for years."

Kade also told me that the dark surroundings, fear of being left alone and the ongoing noise from the TV still circles wildly in his head. It has been almost 48 years since Kade had the last motel room encounter and to this day, he is still suffering in many ways. Each time Kade sat in the salon chair he would often relive his story with me through conversation.

The story of his childhood and upbringing is nothing I could ever imagine. Kade's story is dark, deep and filled with resentment. He is angry, bitter and alone. As he got older the memories of his childhood kept resurfacing. Each time I saw him, I could see the sadness, heartache and shallow look in his eyes. Over time, and now more than four decades later, Kade is consuming lots of alcohol to numb his pain. Furthermore, he is also combining his prescription drugs with his alcohol addiction, and it is evident that he is spiralling down, way down!

I have not seen Kade for more than 12 months. The very last time I saw him he was a broken and fragile man. He looked exhausted! His skin was leathery and showed signs like a road map filled with deep scars! The scars that Kade carries are a reminder of how everything he endured in his childhood have now left him mentally, physically and emotionally depleted and worn out.

> "The greater a child's terror, and the earlier it is experienced, the harder it becomes to develop a strong and healthy sense of self."
> **Nathaniel Brandon**

Mental Health and Addiction

WASTED INHERITANCE

An inheritance that Cissie and Tomo received was like winning the lotto. Straight from Tomo's mouth, "Fu**en wrapped, spendoola baby".

The first time I saw Cissie and Tomo together at the salon was about a week after they were gifted with the money. I was not surprised that they were both high on speed. I did not know them to be any other way, other than flying high on drugs.

Not only did they snort this choice of drug, but they also drank 'speedit' which got its name after they started to sprinkle the white powdery drug into their scotch on ice. Apparently, it's a double whammy and you're extremely high much quicker.

Not ever having enough money for rent was their most common complaint prior to the 'spendoola' and Cissie always dreamt of owning a new car. From the time they inherited all the money, whenever either of them came to the salon all they spoke about was the 'spendoola'. When they spoke, it was always fast-paced, just like the 'speed' they were consuming!

I wondered how long the money would last and if they thought it would be a good idea to pay 12 months' rent in advance, or perhaps they might buy a car or go on a holiday. What about some new clothing? We did discuss all those options and each time they would agree it was a good idea. In fact, we had that same discussion several times. About three months passed, during which both Cissie and Tomo had more pampering sessions than usual in the salon. Having the freedom of spending extra money was no doubt exciting for them and so the salon visits became a regular occurrence.

As it turned out the 'spendoola' gave both Cissie and Tomo leverage to keep living the same lifestyle that they were prior to the money being gifted. The difference was that now, the habit of their drug addiction was on a much bigger scale.

When Cissie said to me one day, "You know that $200 grand we got, fu**, we lived it up. We spent it all on gambling, heaps of sex toys and snorted it right up our nose." Just like that, the money was gone.

Everything they'd always spoken of having like a new car, going on holidays, buying new clothing and paying extra rent, well that just never happened!

WITHERING AWAY

My client Bevan, a gorgeous young man I had known since birth, did not play around with drugs until his very late teenage years.

I had always known Bevan to be polite, well-spoken and hard working. I enjoyed our conversations and thought Bevan was very respectful and friendly when he came into the salon. The entire family were active clients within the salon for more than two decades and are lovely people.

I was so happy for Bevan when he got a girlfriend, his first real love. It was a young love and like many first-time relationships, Bevan's courtship with Lia went pear-shaped within six months. When Bevan and his girlfriend broke up, he found it very difficult to heal. We would often chat about the relationship and in Bevan's mind he was adamant that he would get his girlfriend Lia back and they would end up together again.

Lia was also a client, and her mindset was very different to Bevan's. They were not going to reunite as a couple and that was one thing I knew for sure. It became difficult listening to Bevan, knowing what I had been told by his ex-girlfriend Lia and the worst part was, I couldn't be honest with him. It made me feel terrible!

In our line of work this is often the case – 'knowing everything but knowing nothing'. It gets frustrating at times when you have so much information and there is not a lot you can do with it!

Over time Bevan began to change and his life took a turn for the worse. I found out that suddenly, taking drugs became Bevan's vice! Inhalants, speed and acid trips were just some of the types of drugs that Bevan was experimenting with.

Whenever I saw him, either in the salon or out in the community, I noticed his conversations with me did not make any sense and his words were distorted. Bevan seemed agitated and kept biting his lips. His teeth were constantly chattering, and saliva would slowly ooze out from the side of his mouth. His eyes were glassy, and Bevan looked 20 years older than his 17 years.

The last time I saw Bevan, more than 20 years ago, he was worse for wear. His sunken face, drawn out black eyes and weakened body was so sad to see. I didn't recognise him anymore. I never imagined I would see Bevan turn to drugs, so fast, so hard!

Once again, I witnessed another family within our community become distraught and helpless, as they slowly watched their son deteriorate as a result of drug addiction and substance abuse.

HELP AND EMERGENCY

Are 'you' or 'someone' you know a person who is experiencing any type of abuse or being mistreated in a way that feels unsafe?

If you are in any immediate danger, please reach out and seek help

Australia Call 000

NATIONAL
1800 737 732
www.1800respect.org.au

LIFELINE
13 11 14
www.lifeline.org.au

BEYOND BLUE
1300 224 636
beyondblue.org.au

QLIFE
1800 184 527
qlife.org.au

SUPPORT FOR CHILDREN NATIONAL
1800 55 1800
www.kidshelpline.com.au

Mental Health and Addiction

SUPPORT FOR FAMILIES' NATIONAL RELATIONSHIPS AUSTRALIA
1300 364 277
www.relationships.com.au

SUPPORT FOR MEN NATIONAL MENS LINE AUSTRALIA
1300 789 978
www.mensline.org.au

SUPPORT FOR PEOPLE WITH DISABILITY NATIONAL
National Disability Abuse and Neglect Hotline
1800 880 052

SUPPORT IN YOUR LANGUAGE NATIONAL
Translating and Interpreting Service
131 450
tisnational.gov.au

CHAPTER 5

Your Stories: Sexual Encounters, Interludes and Invitations

BEHIND CLOSED DOORS

One Saturday evening, mid-2011 at the Sydney Hair expo weekend, I met an adorable couple at a bar in Oxford St. It was as though we had known one another for ever.

RiccSTAR my angel had passed away about five months prior and I knew this night was going to be magical for so many different reasons. I wanted to go out for RiccSTAR that evening and with my 'scoobs' ready to blow and my dancing feet excited to move, I knew I was in for a treat!

Unbosoming

Jarryd and Kal were energetic, eccentric and liberating and I thought Kal had such a beautiful aura about him. He was quite mesmerising! They both took me under their wing and wanted to open my eyes to a whole new experience. I let them!

I was curious, excited and not afraid of what was ahead of me. I was completely comfortable spending time with Jarryd and Kal and 'yes' I wanted to look into their world.

It was in the early hours of that Sunday morning when we made our way to 'I do not even know where'! All I knew was that I was in good hands with them. I felt safe.

We proceeded to walk together to our next destination. We casually entered through a very inconspicuous door which led us into a venue. What I can clearly remember is that we walked up two or three flights of stairs. It appeared a little mysterious, dark and secretive, but nevertheless I kept walking.

Once we finally got to the top of the stairs, we were greeted by two beautiful drag queens who looked stunning! I took my jacket off, had a chat with the ladies and yes, I was ready for the unexpected!

To the left of where I was standing were two extremely huge doors. Both Jarryd and Kal were standing on either side of them holding one door handle each. I proceeded to make my way towards them. I stood in the centre of the doors and felt as though something magical was just about to happen!

Jarryd and Kal looked at me and then Kal said, "Are you ready Cathy?" I replied, "Yes". Then Kal asked again, "Are you really ready

Cathy?" I replied, "Yes". Just like that, in what seemed to feel like a slow-motion movement, the doors opened wide and in front of me appeared a paradise of colours.

The room was full of beauty, flamboyancy, feathers, chains, whips, leathers, hairpieces, costumes, sequins, stilettos, stilts, bare skin and music that just made you come alive! I was totally mesmerised! I just stood there, eyes wide open, and after a few minutes of taking it all in, Kal took hold of one hand and with Jarryd holding my other hand, we danced our way through the crowd to get to the other side of the room.

It felt so gratifying. I knew Ricc was right here with me, in this very special moment. I could not take the smile off my face and just kept looking around at everyone and everything in the room. The ambience was unbelievably electrifying.

We then got ourselves a drink at the bar and off I went mingling and meeting people. I found myself a few dance partners and spent the next few hours making my way around the dance floor. I shimmied over to Kal and Jarryd a few times to let them know I was doing just fine and continued to have an amazing time. Absorbing it all was so exhilarating!

I felt at home being in the presence of all those gorgeous people and I will never forget the early hours of that Sunday morning. It felt like being in a story book and I was a part of it!

The culture in the room that evening was clearly all about personal expression and I loved it!

Unbosoming

BOYS' TRIP

The good old boys' club!

Where could I possibly start? They say what happens on the footy trip, stays on the footy trip!

Apparently, on some boys' trips, you are given the green light, the thumbs up that it is okay to fu** around even if you're in a mutual relationship!

How many of these conversations do you think I may have had either in the salon, on a work conference or in general when sitting around with people?

The salon has always been a platform for communication, lots of discussion and plenty of venting. The debates I have had, along with arguments about the secret boys' club topic have been interesting and entertaining. 'Entertaining' because the person with whom I am having the discussion is in fact trying to convince me that this type of behaviour is acceptable! To whom I wonder?

I understand everyone is entitled to their own opinion, but the guys that chat to me about the sexual encounters that take place on a boys trip or boys night out, truly believe that men should be allowed to engage in sexual activities even if they are in a relationship with another person.

I am not saying all men behave this way, but even if they don't engage in any fu**ing around themselves, rest assured many of them will have your back and keep your secret.

Sexual Encounters, Interludes and Invitations

Contrary to what you may believe, I have been told lots of boys' club secrets about sexual encounters. I have grown up in my community of Craigieburn since the age of five and still work in my salon. It is now 33 years of chair, hair and chat. It's fair to say I know a lot of people and lots of personal stories!

Sterling, a long-time client, sits in the salon chair and I know he is going to fill me in on all the gossip about his weekend away. He is a tall man, well-built with a sexy rig and a smile that lights up a room. Just like men check out women, women check out men! If someone looks nice and you feel like complimenting them, I say go for it. I see it as a kind gesture, not an invitation for sex, as some people believe!

Sterling has never been disrespectful to me, nor has he ever hit me up for sex. We have known one another for many years. Sterling was about ten years old when I first started cutting his hair. After 20 years of chatting and lots of haircuts, I became someone that Sterling was very comfortable in disclosing private information to.

On this particular salon visit Sterling starts sharing his stories about the boys' weekend he had recently returned from and informs me of the guys who were badasses who had fu**ed around. He would laugh while he was talking to me thinking that it was funny. He would say things like "Regan and Hunter fu**ed around on their missus and they would not have a clue". He would find it entertaining and would keep laughing. On many occasions, Sterling was also a badass himself and told me over and over that he was proud of his fu**ing around! He would often say, "What you don't know won't hurt you".

Peyton on the other hand is lovely and has been the besotted girlfriend of Sterling for more than three years. They have a little baby now and are still in a relationship. I am sure to this day Peyton still has no idea about all the sexual encounters Sterling has indulged in!

Although Sterling believes he is the answer to every woman's dream, when he constantly feeds me his stories, the reality is, in my head, I am thinking, "What an asshole!"

I often reply with, "Seriously Sterling, you're a fu**wit. You seriously cannot believe that the bullshit that's dribbling out of your mouth right now is normal and or justified." He laughs at me!

Sterling has always been living his best life, the 'I want my cake and want to eat it too' kind of life. I have no doubt there are many others who believe that this is their way of living their best life.

What I have learnt is that the conversions I have had with males about affairs and sexual encounters have made me feel less intimidated by men, and more inclined to stand up to them.

In true salon form, I know everything, but know nothing.

DELUSIONAL

When my client Draco says to me, "I'd love to take you out for dinner and drinks sometime", in my head I'm thinking "as if"!

What the fu**! What amuses me the most is not only am I married, but so is Draco. I know his wife and Draco knows my husband. Our kids played local sport together, and I know he fu**ed around behind his wife's back because he had told me on more than one occasion.

Draco travels for work and is away from home for weeks at a time. There have been many conversations where Draco has confided in me about his flings with other women, and he thinks it's a not big deal if his wife Petra doesn't know.

I have known Draco long enough to tell him how much of a shitty person he is, but he just looks at me with a smile and continues to laugh. When I ask him why he is laughing he will stare at me in the mirror and say, "What is the problem?" as though it is not a problem at all.

Whenever I cross paths with Draco and Petra together on the weekends, he will smile at me and act as though he is the picture-perfect husband! I smile and greet them both as though I do not know a thing, and although I know a lot, my silence remains.

Being in Draco's presence isn't always an enjoyable experience. At times it is a complete turn-off!

Thank fu** he doesn't live in my community anymore. I'm so relieved to know that Draco had to venture on to another salon!

Hopefully he doesn't ask his new hair stylist on a dinner date!

EXCLUSIVE INVITE

Out of the blue Candy says, "I love going to swingers' parties, you should join us sometime. Come on, just one time."

Unbosoming

I was invited by Candy to attend a gathering at a hidden location for an 'all-in, anything goes, adult event'. I politely declined.

I was not afraid of what I may have experienced; it just had not been on my radar as a bucket list thing to do. I am a curious person who may take risks at times, but this just didn't draw me in. Candy kept trying to convince me that I would be fine, and that I didn't have to participate in any sexual activities unless I chose to. I just wasn't interested.

Apparently if I decided to attend, there were rules I needed to abide by:

1) These gatherings took place in Melbourne, this I did know. The exact location of the event would not be revealed until 5pm on that day, and you had a code to adhere to. Being ready was paramount as was arriving within a certain time frame. If you missed the deadline, too bad, doors got locked.

2) Dress code was anything that took your fancy, although you couldn't rock up naked. You may have been bare skin under your jacket, yes, but you had to arrive covered up!

3) You didn't have to be in a relationship; however, you did have to arrive as a couple; one male and one female. This rule was purely to even out numbers of both sexes.

4) Once you were through the doors, you needed to leave your inhibitions behind and be extremely open-minded about whatever you may encounter next!

5) The last and most important rule of these sex parties was that the male partner (whom you arrived with), could only

engage in sexual activity after the female he attended with participated first!

I am not entirely sure what such a night would have been like. I never agreed to join Candy on this sexual adventure, even though I would love to have been a fly on the wall! All I know is what I have been told by Candy, and it's pretty damn sexy and wild!

HARLEY RIDE

"Interested in coming on a Harley ride with me some day? We can stop at a bar and grab a drink and some lunch." I reply, "Um, no thanks!"

This guy, Wally, is a wonderful man! We could always have a laugh together, our conversations were great and his mum, Lilli, was so kind and lovely. I always thought of Wally as a top bloke, and I genuinely enjoyed my time with him at the salon.

Whenever Wally came in to get a haircut, he always asked me to go on a Harley ride with him. I would just laugh and say, "You're dreaming, Wally". The truth is, we were always polite and respectful to one another whenever we caught up in the salon. And although I was single at the time, quite frankly I just wasn't interested in anything other than a professional relationship with Wally.

Each time I saw Wally for his monthly haircut, he would tell me he was with a new woman. In all the time I knew him, I actually do not think he was ever in a full-on loving relationship. Although he had lots of different women in his life, to me it seemed like he had a need or craving to always have a companion around, someone by his side. For some reason, the women didn't seem to stay around for long, and I began to wonder why. Whenever I asked Wally about his relationships and why they did not work out, he would always just say they were not right for him.

Wally's mum Lilli was a treat and adored her son. She thought he could do no wrong. Lilli would often say to me, "Oh it would be so good if you could go out on a date with my boy".

Each time I would cut Wally's hair, he would always bring up the same invitation for that bike ride, and I would always decline the offer and tell him to get over it! Then he'd reply with, "Nah, alright, I know you're not into motorbikes. What about going on a dinner date with me?" I would always be polite and would not entertain his invite. A credit to Wally, he persistently asked me out, without success.

About five years ago, I bumped into Lilli on an outing and hadn't seen either her nor Wally for such a long time. Lilli told me that Wally got married to a lovely woman named Cora, and that together they have three beautiful children. I was so happy to see Lilli and even happier knowing that Wally finally found a woman to love. Lilli also told me that Wally is loving life on the Sunshine Coast with his family and she has never seen him happier!

Lovely Lilli has since passed away. I adored this woman, and she adored her son like a precious jewel. I will always remember Wally as a beautiful soul and I am so happy that he found true and meaningful love with Cora.

Wally had a big heart and I have no doubt that he is a wonderful dad.

Sexual Encounters, Interludes and Invitations

KEEP IT PRIVATE

Zeke was a such womaniser. He was never shy in being upfront about his sexual antics, and at times I thought, "Seriously, that's way too much information!"

Zeke would come out and say, "I love it when my wife dresses up in her nurse's outfit, what a turn on!" He would then insist that I look at pictures of his wife, Aspen, in her outfit! I would always shut him down quickly and would tell him to put his phone away.

"Yes, I get it Zeke, dress ups in the bedroom can be fun. What I don't like is that you are wanting to share your intimate bedroom moments with me by showing me Aspen in her outfit."

I am sure Zeke thought I would get turned on when he shared his personal information with me, but the truth is, it was a turn-off! My thoughts were, "If I am your stylist and you decide to share images of your partner in her playful, sexy costume, seriously, that's just fu**ed up! I'm not interested!"

I would not appreciate my partner sharing private images of me, and I could not imagine Aspen thinking it was appropriate for her husband to share these images of her. To make it worse, Aspen was my client! I found it difficult to block out shit like this.

Worst part is that when I was in the presence of Zeke and Aspen together, it made me feel awkward. Knowing that Zeke wanted to show me private images of Aspen was really degrading and offensive. It's just not right, period!

There are a lot of personal truths confessed within our workplace, and I wholeheartedly understand that it is important to maintain a level of professionalism. But fu**, it is so hard knowing what you know and not being able to give people the heads up.

If you believe that disclosing intimate, sexual images to another person is acceptable, I beg to differ! It's wrong on so many levels. Respect yourself and your loved ones.

LOLLIPOP

Floyd is a gay man who I have only known for a few years. He is eccentric, loud, unpredictable and very obnoxious, especially when he is drunk. He has always shared very explicit information with me. Not much has surprised me except the time he proceeded to give me insight into his new world.

This conversation came out of the blue and took me completely by surprise! Floyd told me that he was making easy money for little work. I was wondering, "How is that so? What is the secret to easy money without working hard?"

What I heard next was not what I was expecting. Floyd said to me, "I've been giving head jobs to men, sucking di** and getting paid big dollars". He went on to tell me that most of the guys are married men! He continued to tell me that the men he was involved with were generally ethnic European men, who came from very religious backgrounds. I asked him how he met these men and how this chapter in his life started.

Floyd was married for more than ten years and lost his husband to an illness. Months and months had gone by, and he was feeling very isolated and lonely. He decided to put himself out there by joining a dating site and gave himself a profile name, 'Lollipop'. He signed up to a website predominately for gay men. Floyd told me that it was very easy to meet up with other men who wanted quick and discrete sexual favours. I asked where he would meet these men and where the encounters took place. As it turns out, most of his rendezvous took place in local community parks and sporting reserves, in broad daylight! Men who wanted to be extra secretive would book hotel rooms.

Coming home from the city one evening, Floyd offered oral sex to his taxi driver in lieu of money. The older taxi driver accepted the offer and blew his load within minutes. I kid you not, this is exactly what Floyd told me! This taxi driver became Floyd's regular chauffeur, and the sexual encounters continued.

Some people are more what they hide than what they show, and you wouldn't know any different!

NAKED

I had known Rayland for 25 years, and although most of the time he was friendly, there were times when he acted like a real fu**wit! He was way too confident and believed that when he walked into the salon, we drooled over him. I have no issue paying a compliment to others, but with Rayland I never felt that I needed to give him any more attention. He brought way too much attention to himself!

Unbosoming

Rayland was always well-groomed and very self-assured, but his stories got a little boring after a while. His conversations were always about women, money and his cars. He had travelled all over the world and loved living in the fast lane; cocaine was his biggest habit! He had plenty of money, and I think Rayland believed his cash could buy anything, and that he was in control of everyone and everything! Rayland did not hesitate or hold back about what he told me, and a lot of the time his stories came with way too much information.

I was cutting his hair one day, and through the mirror I could see him staring at a staff member in an unusual way. I started to feel uncomfortable and a little weirded out!

He was always high on cocaine and I did not care about that, but on this day, I looked up and asked him, "What are you staring at?" He laughed and replied, "I was imagining that Sharni was naked". My immediate thoughts were, "What a fu**ing pig, who even says that!"

I looked up again, stared at him eye-to-eye through the mirror and replied, "Seriously Rayland, that's just fu**ed up and you're crossing the line now. I don't give a shit about the personal crap you feed me all the time, but do not ever make remarks or comments like that to me again about anyone in my workplace." Immediately Rayland replied, "Oh I'm only fu**ing around with you. It's a joke, don't take it too serious!"

Within a few seconds, the conversation changed very quickly. I tried to remain calm and composed. I washed Rayland's hair, towel dried it and did not speak a word. Nor did Rayland.

We walked to the register and when Rayland was ready to pay for his haircut, I refused the money. I told him that I was really turned off by what he had said, and that I didn't want his money. I just wanted him to leave.

No more than ten minutes later the salon phone rang. When I answered it, I recognised it was Rayland's voice. He was very apologetic and said he felt bad about what he had said to me about my employee. I replied, "Apology accepted, Rayland, can't talk now as I need to get back to my client. Enjoy the rest of your day."

Three weeks later, Rayland made an appointment and came to the salon. He walked in as though what happened last time didn't happen! I greeted him, smiled, put my big girl pants on, stood tall, and let my professionalism take over!

The conversation about his last visit at the salon didn't come up. It was business as usual.

Sometimes you must accept that some, not all, people will act like shitty humans.

At times you need to stop trying to see the good in them that isn't there.

NAUGHTY THOUGHTS

I was caught off guard one day when a regular client, Drake, asked me if I thought badly of him because he had just told me that he was having naughty thoughts and naughty dreams about one of my staff members.

I just looked at him and said, "What the fu**. I can't believe you just told me that considering I am more than just your hairdresser. I am good friends with your wife as well and it just feels a little weird that you just said that to me."

Drake laughed and changed the conversation very quickly and thank goodness he did as it made me feel uncomfortable.

When Drake left the salon I told my staff member what had just happened and her reaction was, "Oh yuck, I am extremely creeped out by what Drake said. I always knew he was a womaniser but now that just makes me dislike him even more."

My staff member proceeded to tell me that she does not like it when Drake comes into the salon and that when he walks through the door it is as though the world has to stand still and he wants us to make a fuss about him. It is one thing to be polite and greet your clients as they enter the salon, and it is another thing to stop everything you are doing just to make Drake's presence be known, like he expects.

My team and I are so glad that Drake is not a client anymore!

We all have thoughts or dreams whatever they may be but sometimes saying nothing is best, as opposed to sharing too much.

ONE NIGHT STAND-REVISITED

It was a sad time when I found out that Kerri's mum, Joni, had passed away. I had known Joni, who was such a wonderful woman, for over 30 years, and I always adored her zest for life. Whenever she came to the salon, I enjoyed chatting with her. This gorgeous woman always had a happy-go-lucky attitude, and it broke my heart when I found out that she did not pull through the operation.

Sexual Encounters, Interludes and Invitations

A few weeks after Joni had passed away, sitting in front of me in the chair for his monthly haircut was Marty, Kerri's husband. He 'threw me for a six' with what he told me!

I understood Marty's wife was busy, preoccupied taking care of her mum during a very difficult time, but I had no idea what mess Marty had gotten himself into.

To be frank, I wasn't a fan of Marty. In fact, I didn't enjoy our conversations. I am not sure why, but he always seemed a little eerie. Whenever we spoke, he would not directly look at me, not even through the mirror. There was never eye contact between us.

Marty began to tell me that Kerri wasn't paying attention to him and that he felt neglected, because all that Kerri did was put time and energy into caring for her mum. He went on to tell me that to make himself feel better, he became involved with another woman. My immediate thoughts were, "You selfish bastard! Your wife was caring for her sick mother and you're getting yourself a quick fu** from another person. What the fu**!"

Marty proceeded to tell me that he felt guilty about his actions, and as much as he still loved his wife Kerri, he also had feelings for the other woman. He asked me to promise not to tell his wife Kerri what I knew. I told Marty that day that the conversations that happen within the salon walls, stay within the salon walls.

Marty also told me that he fu**ed up, but he couldn't help himself. He wanted to maintain the relationship with the other woman.

We all make mistakes and in some cases just like Marty, continue to keep making those same mistakes.

And yet again, knowing what I know makes it extremely difficult, especially because I also have a relationship with Kerri, who has no idea what her husband told me. Marty and Kerri are still married!

PARTY BOAT

We were in Darling Harbour at a work function in Sydney, and the party boat was rocking in more ways than one! Everyone was having fun. We were all dancing, drinking, partying, and some of us even shared a few happy 'scoobs' on the deck.

It was such a great vibe and the night was gearing up in more ways than one. Everyone was having a ball. In true Cathy style, you will always find me ripping up the dance floor, boogying the night away, enjoying the freedom of music, movement and feeling as free as a bird.

Unexpectedly, someone came up to me from behind and buried their head into my neck. The movement was slow and seductive, and I felt a body get close to mine. Suddenly a woman's voice whispered into my ear, "Would you be interested in having an intimate time with me tonight? I find you to be very attractive, I've been watching you all night. Let's leave together and go back to my hotel when the boat docks."

I gently turned around, looked at her and smiled. I had never met this woman before. I gave her a hug, and replied, "Thanks for the invite, you're beautiful!" Then I took her hand and said, "Would you like to meet my husband?" We introduced ourselves, and together with Giselle we had a chat and then both smiled at one another. I had a dance with her, who I must say was enchanting to look at. Then I gave her another hug and we went our separate ways.

I told my hubby about the proposal I had just gotten and he asked me if he was invited. I replied, "It was a solo invitation, Frankie!"

As it turned out Giselle also gave a mutual friend of mine, Saraya, a similar proposal as my husband and I watched on. Only difference was Saraya's husband Austin was absolutely gutted that another woman had given his wife some female attention. Austin suddenly became defensive. He exchanged nasty words with Giselle, and it wasn't pleasant. Austin's behaviour was disgusting and degrading.

Frank and I had no hesitation stepping in to ask Austin to calm the fu** down. Seriously, it was not as though Saraya and Giselle had an intimate kiss or went off to a corner of the boat for privacy. The evening turned sour, and an unexpected proposal ended with unwarranted, unnecessary hostility!

Dear Strong Women: You are not intimidating, he is intimidated. There's a difference.
www.livelifehappy.com

PLAYING GAMES

Aylli is a smart businesswoman who works alongside her co-founder in a very successful company. You cannot help but notice Aylli when she is in your direct vision. She is tall with a stylish walk and an upright posture, and along with her confidence that makes this woman eye-catching. Seriously, what a stunner! Eye candy!

Whenever Aylli would walk through the salon doors, heads turned. Everyone would quickly look at her in a way that did not seem obvious, but you knew they all wanted to check her out. And they did!

Unbosoming

When she came in for a salon visit on this particular day I told her how stunning she looked. Aylli replied with, "I always dress like this for my business partner, he loves it. We have play dates at work and act out sexual pleasures. We have been having sex for over a year now, and my husband does not have a problem with it."

Aylli is not alone when it comes to workplace rendezvous. I have heard similar stories just like this and apparently it is quite common for these behaviours to occur in a workplace setting!

Whenever I catch up with Aylli, it is definitely an interesting and saucy conversation. She is like an open book and is very self-assured. From the first time we met, Aylli hasn't changed and is not afraid to speak her truth.

Having a family is not on Aylli's agenda and living her life this way mutually suits both her and her husband.

On one occasion, Aylli told me that she has great sex with Christo, her husband, as a result of her being sexually active with another man.

Every now and then, Aylli, Christo, and her work colleague, Ryder, attend business events together. They also dine out and go away on vacations as a threesome!

If I told you that Christo has been present many times watching his wife Aylli and Ryder together, would you believe it to be true?

True it is!

SEX ADDICT

When I was confronted unexpectedly with "I'm a sex addict", it led me to an extended chat in the chair. I had an hour to spare and was so intrigued by what Marni had said.

Our conversation became very much a lesson in learning, well for me anyway! I was mind blown by all the different terminology associated to this kind of addiction, 'sexual addiction'. I honestly wasn't aware that spiritual sex, trauma-based sex, psychological sex, biological sex, just to name a few, were all behaviours of this addiction. I was so curious that I asked Marni to continue explaining more.

Marni and her sexual encounter stories were streamy, erotic, seductive and in many ways, concerning! Everything that Marni told me that day was filled with explicit detail, and I was astonished at how many sexual partners she had been involved with.

As the discussion continued, I was beginning to feel worried about Marni and her state of mind. I asked her if she felt safe when she was with these different sexual partners, and if there were any times where she was in danger. I was not surprised when Marni replied with, "Yes there have been many times that I have felt afraid". She also told me that her addiction overpowered her mind and that she could not stop herself from engaging in sexual activities.

To my surprise, what I also found out during this discussion was that this is a real issue and that it's impacting the lives of millions of individuals globally! If you are a little naïve as I was at the time, sex addiction behaviours can be anything from internet porn, fetishes and self-masturbation. In many individuals, but not all, this addiction can contribute to compulsive, life-destroying patterns that can damage and affect relationships, families and friendships.

Marni realised in time that it was not fair to her, or her husband, to keep their relationship going and after only three years of marriage, they decided to divorce. Marni took ownership that the breakdown of her marriage was purely a result of her addiction, cravings and ongoing dependency on sex. Along with her past experiences, it made her realise that remaining single would best suit her needs and her addiction.

There were many times I would witness Marni became emotional. I sensed a deep heartache and felt her loneliness. It made me sad looking into her eyes.

As I continue to listen and learn I am more aware that any one of us can be subjected to addiction. Any kind of addiction does not discriminate.

STRIP CLUB

I was always so curious about female strip clubs, so on a night out with some friends, we decided to go and see what really happens in these bars.

What I did notice, was that the women who worked there did not like us girls in their space. That was evident.

When I looked around, it was like watching lots of older men act like they had never been around women before. They sat in their chairs as though they were kings, showcasing their dollar bills whilst the women were working their magic and making money.

Sexual Encounters, Interludes and Invitations

Looking around, there were also a lot of young guys in the venue. As usual, my curiosity kicked in and I began to chat with them.

I asked questions like:
"What is all the hype about in these clubs?"
"Why do you come to these clubs and how often?"
"Are you married?"
"Do you have partners?"
"How much money do you spend in the club?"
"Can you get exclusive one on one attention?"
"Are there private rooms here in the club for private sessions?"

Being amongst all these people and watching was so fu**ing interesting, for so many reasons!

Some of the responses I got included:

"It's a guy thing, men have always gone to strip clubs."
"It's just a bit of fun, a laugh."
"It's a bucks night."
"My missus wouldn't have a clue that I come here."
"Money gets action… hahaha."
"I come here every week. Sassy the dancer on stage now is exclusively mine."

At one point during the night, I decided to sit right up toward the stage in front of the pole dancing table. The female dancer was not impressed. I casually sat and watched what was happening around me, and I can confirm, lots of dollar bills were free flowing! The men around me were of all ages and were vying for attention and in that moment, they got it…at a cost!

We stayed at the bar a few hours and had some intriguing conversations. What I did find interesting was, some of the men actually thought they were going to be taking my friends and I home for a session....... THAT WAS CLEARLY NEVER GOING TO HAPPEN.

SNOW WHITE HAIR

In October 1988 I became friends with the most kind-hearted woman. Her presence was an aura of vibrancy and her smile and laughter engulfed me each time we were together.

We shared some of the best times within the salon and as a small community we pretty much knew everyone. I was 18 years of age and Prynnie was 30 years my senior. Despite our age difference we got on like 'a house on fire'!

We were both chatterboxes and spoke about everything and anything. We would often hang out at the salon after work hours and catch up on our day. I smoked cigarettes back then and it was a daily routine for me to have my coffee and a ciggy or ten, before heading home each night.

I learnt a lot from Prynnie over two decades and was in awe of her Snow White hair. It was as icy as snow and suited her beautifully. Getting to know Prynnie on a personal level was interesting and exciting. Her energy was infectious and the banter we shared was fu**ing awesome. Prynnie would always crack a joke and make me laugh hysterically and I loved her for that.

Aside from the beautiful soul that Prynnie was, clearly for me it was her work ethic and ongoing resilience that inspired me the most. She had a job as a local cleaner and her days would begin very early. This involved both a morning and an afternoon shift and it was physically hard work with early starts and late finishes.

Prynnie was a mother to four children. Her daughters Shaylyn and Dakota were around the same age as me and her two sons Colby and Easton were younger. Throughout those two decades I got to know each of them and became their local hairdresser. I also got to meet two of Prynnie's son in laws and over time met some of her grandchildren.

Up until now, all of Prynnie's children and grandchildren have been lovely and shown respect towards me. Her granddaughter Chelle has always stood out to me. She has an infectious smile and is really polite. There is a pure gentleness within Chelle that I see, and which to me is a reflection of her nan.

One thing for sure is that Prynnie always spoke highly of her children and her grandchildren. Even when she was being confronted with family issues and challenges, she would always continue to tell me how much she loved her family. This never changed as long as I knew Prynnie.

What did change was the intimate encounters that Prynnie started to have with her daughter's husband! Shaylyn was Prynnie's eldest daughter and a wonderful woman who I got to know in the salon when I did her hair. To this day I have never spoken to Shaylyn about what I know and unless it is bought to my attention from Shaylyn, clearly there is nothing to discuss.

It definitely came as a surprise to me when Prynnie confessed that she had feelings for Baxter, her son-in-law. I became really concerned about Prynnie and what she had just told me. It was a danger zone situation! As much as we were great friends and spoke openly about so many personal issues, I truly had no idea that Prynnie had developed sincere feelings for Baxter. From what she told me, Baxter also had feelings for Prynnie.

Was this real love?

The sexual encounters that Prynnie and Baxter were sharing together was really happening, and it was not right! It was alarming and dangerous on so many levels and in time Prynnie came to realise that what was going on was wrong.

Over time Prynnie began to distance herself from me and the salon. It was as though she was ashamed of what I knew. As much as I reassured her that I was there to support her, deep down I sensed that she had a lot of remorse, regret and embarrassment about what she had done.

Time went on as though the world stood still and the intimate encounter that Prynnie and Baxter shared was never discussed with me again.

Prynnie and I moved on in life travelling in different directions. Our relationship organically faded out. We never revisited the conversation of her intimate encounter and just got on with our lives.

Whenever we saw one another at the shop we would always make time to stop and talk. We would give each other a kiss hello and embrace with a hug as we always did. It was a quick chat about our family and making sure everyone was well and then off we would go our separate way.

What I knew stayed with me and I told no one of this, literally no one!

Out of the blue one day at the salon, only just recently, the story of Prynnie and her intimate encounter with Baxter came to the forefront of a conversation that an employee had brought to my attention. I allowed my employee to just keep talking as I listened. Clearly everything I knew was out in the open and some of Prynnie's family members were aware of what had happened in her personal life many years ago.

I told my employee that I knew, and she looked at me with a bewildered face, as though in shock! I told her it was true and that Prynnie and Baxter were intimately involved and that despite what I knew, my feelings towards Prynnie have never changed.

I will always remember the great times I spent with Prynnie, the laughs we shared and the many conversations we had.

Prynnie passed in July 2020 at the age of 81 and is now a flying angel in the skies above.

THE AFFAIR

In a salon environment it is common to hear about people's lives and their personal experiences and stories. As a hairdresser I can tell you there is no holding back with what is expressed in conversation, especially when it comes to intimacy and relationships.

One day whilst giving Malakai a haircut, he said, "I've been fu**ing one of my work colleagues for a while now. It's the release I need for putting up with shit from Camilla. She is such a bitch."

I replied, "Seriously Malakai, if hooking up and fu**ing around because Camilla pissed you off makes you feel good, well, you're an asshole! Why don't you just end your marriage and move on?"

Malakai not only fu**s around, he also throws his weight around. Camilla's face tells a story. I have also been a witness to Malakai's verbal abuse in the salon on more than one occasion.

Malakai is a traditional, old-school European man, who has views that are a little backwards. I had known him for several years, and I always thought he was arrogant. Salon conversations were always about how he got to enjoy days out with his mates and weekend getaways with the boys. Pretty much his life seemed to be all that he wanted it to be. The freedom to be him!

He would often tell me that he only wanted Camilla to wear a certain style of clothing, and that a night out with the girls was out of the question. Fu** right off with your views, you old-school fu**wit! I loathe men like this!

When a wife is being controlled in this manner, it can be a recipe for a lifetime of secret sadness. These women may seem happy on the surface, but underneath tells a whole different story. Being controlled by your husband, and pleasing him like he is your master, is what many women endure, often out of fear or insecurity.

Just like my own marriage, most of us in relationships will be faced with dramas and arguments. It's normal to have disagreements and not always see eye to eye on everything.

There are many times that my husband and I will agree to disagree, just so that we can move on. In fact, I don't actually agree all the time, neither does he but it's easier to put things behind you or the drama could last way longer than it needs to.

We should be able to have our own thoughts and voice our own opinions, whilst still being respectful towards each other.

Unfortunately, I know way too many women in relationships with men who 'rule the roost' and 'wear the pants'. So many stories about toxic relationships have been shared with me over the past three decades, and many times these women have tried to justify their partner's behaviour by blaming themselves! These women have told me that their partners repeatedly get into their head and make them believe it's their fault they were beaten and cheated on. These women are threatened that if they speak about it to anyone, there will be consequences! To top it off, many of these women have also told me that they've been gifted with money, new cars, expensive gifts and holidays to keep their turbulent relationships a secret.

Sexual abuse, domestic violence and financial abuse are just some of the destructive and destroying issues people are facing each day in their relationships! These harmful and damaging issues have always been spoken of in my family home, to inform and educate one another about what is and isn't acceptable when maintaining healthy and fulfilling relationships.

As my kids were growing up and still to this day, I never hesitated to discuss real issues such as domestic violence and abuse. Many times, I had people tell me that my kids were too young to know too much, or that what I told them wasn't appropriate. I beg to differ!

It is our responsibility to talk more openly about respectful relationships, respect for self and that abusive relationships are a 'no go zone'. These conversations should be encouraged at home, at school and within the wider community so that we can better educate ourselves.

WHO'S THE MOLE?

As a young 18-year-old Miguel was, in my opinion, naïve, immature and extremely vulgar in so many ways.

He was having lots of sex with lots of girls and when Miguel told me he ended up with an STD (Sexual Transmitted Disease), I was not shocked or surprised.

In Miguel's words, "I got an STD from a dirty mole I have been having sex with". As he was telling me, he was laughing.

I asked him why he was laughing and what was so funny about having an STD and he replied, "Whatever, I don't care, I am also fu**ing a few other moles on the side and don't give a shit about what happens".

I replied, "You're nasty Miguel, you are giving everyone else an STD as well by messing around with so many different girls. That is so careless and totally a terrible thing to be doing." Miguel just laughed at me as though everything I said was a funny joke.

Aside from transmitting the STD, Miguel was also referring to all the girls he was having sex with as 'dirty moles'. I found his behaviour and what he was saying to be absolutely disgusting! He was disgusting!

I am so glad that Miguel's family didn't stay in Craigieburn for very long. I was not keen on having Miguel or his chauvinistic dad Ivanko return to the salon!

Practising safe sex is imperative to your wellbeing and the wellbeing of others. Make it a priority to look after yourself. You are important. Respect your body.

We also have a responsibility and a moral conscience to others to inform them of sexual health issues that may have an impact on them.

WINK

Albert is a man on a mission. I think his mission is to impress other women. When he talks to me about his personal sexual ideas I just think, "Really, shut the fu** up!"

When Albert says, "Hey Cathy do you think I should buy my wife lingerie as a treat? It might get her going, you know what I mean?" I reply, "No Albert, I don't know what you mean". Then he winks at me and smiles.

Here is a man with lingerie on his mind, sexy women images on his phone and loving that someone is in his personal space touching his hair whilst getting it cut. In the context of this conversation, it seemed a little perverted and it made me feel a little uncomfortable, especially the wink!

Albert kept talking and was excited to let me know he had a plan to surprise his wife Tia. He wanted to buy her sexy lingerie and wanted my opinion on size, colour and style. I was comfortable in giving him some ideas on what to purchase for his Tia. The wink, however, was something else. What was that about? I became a little weirded out after that.

To top it off, Albert read me a couple of the messages he and his Tia had exchanged. Seriously? This is fu**ing next level, a 'NO' go zone. But yes, this is what happened.

As the haircut service continued, I remained calm and professional. I knew Albert well and politely told him to put his phone away and keep his messages private. I then proceeded to tell Albert that a friendly assistant in a lingerie store would be able to meet his needs with purchasing the gift he was looking for.

The wink Albert gave me and the personal messages he divulged felt wrong on so many levels. Aside from that, Tia is a regular client at the salon, who I have known quite well and have a mutual relationship with. That makes it even more repulsive!

X 2 WOMEN FOR SUGAR DADDY

I had only been a qualified hairdresser and business owner for six months when I met Nevie. At first glance you could tell that she was under the influence of drugs and some days Nevie looked unwell and 'worse for wear'. Although Nevie was always extremely friendly and polite I would notice that her behavioural pattern changed, and I never knew what to expect when she visited the salon. Would she be crying, laughing, vomiting or totally 'away with the fairies'?

I was oblivious to how Nevie lived her life until one day I was invited into a conversation about her secretive world. Nevie was a prostitute and had been living her life this way for nearly eight years.

Unquestionably, it was a time when I learnt a lot about what people do to survive in this world. For many there are struggles, setbacks, trauma and mental health issues, as well as other issues that force people to sometimes do the unexpected!

Nevie continued to tell me that her life went from rags to riches when she met Remy and that this is when her life began to change for the better.

Remy was one of Nevie's clients. He turned out to be her exclusive man. Whenever Nevie spoke about him, she would refer to Remy as her sugar daddy.

As the months went on, I noticed that Nevie started to look healthier, happier and on top of the world. I loved seeing her and noticed that our conversations flowed better.

The proposal that Nevie accepted from Remy was in her words "a lucky break". There was no more prostitution work for Nevie and no other men in her life. Remy wanted Nevie, exclusively, to himself, and he got what he wanted.

In return for being the woman in Remy's life, Nevie was gifted with a new apartment in the city, her son's school fees were taken care of and Remy also bought Nevie a new car. It did not stop there. Nevie was also constantly spoilt with clothes, money and jewellery amongst other things.

The only thing left to say about sugar daddy Remy is that he was a wealthy businessman who was also married. He had three children of his own and was having his cake and eating it too. Not uncommon!

As for Nevie I hope that she is happy, healthy and flourishing with or without Remy.

CHAPTER 6

Your Stories: Violence, Harassment and Abuse

Memories are the roots of your life and traumatic memories will hide like a shadow in the brain. For many these memories can't be consciously accessed and eventually those suppressed memories can cause debilitating psychological problems.

DISCREET FUNDING

Abigail was a woman who knew how to cover her tracks. She also knew how to cover her bruises!

It was in 1990 when I first met with Abigail. At face value, she appeared to be confident, self-assured and was always well-groomed. Her weekly blow wave service was ongoing for years and there was never a shortage of information when it came to Abigail sharing her life story. She wasn't afraid to let me know about her past. Each time we saw one another I learnt more about her and what happened when she was growing up.

As a young girl Abigail was a victim of domestic violence and sexual abuse and sadly her childhood experiences continued to traumatise her as an adult. From week to week, Abigail was in her own 'survival mode'. Her moods spiralled up and down and played out differently whenever I saw her. The amount of heroin Abigail consumed determined the mood she was in and even then, it chopped and changed constantly.

It was interesting listening to Abigail speak but it was very confronting, especially when she would momentarily hold her sunglasses down so that I could see her eyes. They were bruised, swollen and to the right of her forehead was a nasty gash. When I asked Abigail if she was feeling okay and if there was anything I could do to help her, she replied promptly with, "Don't worry about me love, it's not the first time and won't be the last. Shady is a bastard and I am used to getting a beating."

Shady is Abigail's partner and his name suits him perfectly. As Abigail kept talking, she lifted her glasses back up and was smiling. She also had a smug look on her face. I wasn't sure why she was smiling but I could sense that her fighting spirit was directed against Shady, and it was as though she had a vendetta against him. I was scared for her! Her defensive mechanism seemed as though she was in control, but her black eyes told a very different story.

I knew about Shady and his corruptive lifestyle not only from what Abigail had told me but what others had also shared with me in conversation. For years Shady has been up to all sorts of illegal mishaps and was well-known within our community. Everything I was told by Abigail over the years replicated what I already knew. Making lots of illegal money and receiving the dole as a top up was how Shady and Abigail supported their lifestyle. They were both happily receiving welfare payments and so were many others who were a part of their corruptive circle of acquaintances.

Although Shady was always nice to me, I also knew how to be nice back. I had been repeatedly warned not to ask Shady too many questions when he got a haircut. Whenever he popped into the salon he would do so without having made a booking. He would literally come in and want his hair done straight away. My staff were not keen on cutting his hair and made this known to me. I always did my best to suit Shady and in most cases, it turned out to be a quick and easy haircut. Thank goodness for that because Shady's presence never felt warm and engaging.

One day Abigail told me that she was secretly hiding her money by keeping it in a betting account. I asked why? Abigail replied, "So that I can have my own money without Shady knowing about it".

In the back of my mind I was totally aware of how Shady mistreated Abigail and often wondered how she stayed in a relationship with him. Not only did Shady physically and sexually abuse Abigail, he also had many other women in his life. Abigail was aware of his affairs.

Drug trafficking, cash and corruption go hand in hand. I have no doubt this exchange of unlawful activity is and will always remain in society!! Money laundering and drug distribution has been happening for as long as I can remember and Abigail's story is similar to others I have heard. The only difference with Abigail's story is her hiding place. I hadn't ever heard of anyone stashing their money in a betting account and I hope that Shady never found out about her secret!

Further to Abigail's life experiences, as an eight-year-old, innocent, young girl, she had been violated by an older man. He was a family member. As she got older those childhood experiences continued to haunt and traumatise Abigail.

I last saw Abigail when she was about 58 years old and that was more than eight years ago. Her face looked like a map of life and the deep creases on her skin appeared heavy and scarred. The sadness in her eyes was obvious.

Just like Abigail there are many women who are in abusive and toxic relationships. My hope is that as a society right now in the present and moving forward into the future, we continue to educate and empower young girls and woman about the importance of stopping violence against women.

ELEVATOR MAN

An industry event that I attended more than 15 years ago turned sour when I was confronted with an unexpected incident.

Alongside work colleagues and company representatives we were enjoying a private function in one of Sydney's five-star hotels. Mingling and networking was great and like previous events I had attended, it was turning out to be a fun night.

Riccstar was with me and we were having such a fabulous time. Ricc was loving the surroundings and the people he was meeting.

He felt like he was amongst the elite and just like everyone else, we were celebrating our hairdressing industry in style. Dressed to impress and all glammed up we were in our element.

The banter that Truc and Ricc were revelling in had us in belly-aching laughter. They were both hilariously funny and I knew Ricc was having an absolute whale of a time. He had not been involved in corporate events for years and he was loving it as he was working the room with his magical smile. Everyone was loving Riccstar and that was evident.

The hospitality of the corporate company was impeccable. The team were fascinating, inviting and very down to earth. I always loved being in the presence of such friendly people and looked forward to catching up with the same crew at each event.

Later in the evening when the function was over a few of us decided to kick on and go for a 'night cap'. As we made our plan and gathered our belongings one by one, we went our separate ways. Some went back to their hotel rooms to change shoes or freshen up while others waited in the foyer.

We had a meeting time and destination and Ricc and I were looking forward to partying on. Ricc had left with a few of the others and I quickly made my way to the restroom. As I came out of the restroom, a guy from the function was in the foyer. We proceeded to make our way to meet the others. We began talking as we walked into the elevator and once the doors closed that was when a turn of events made me feel threatened and uncomfortable. The 'elevator man' pushed me up against the corner of the small space we were in and tried to kiss me. He pushed his body up against mine and had a hold on me that felt invasive and forceful. Immediately I felt like

I was in danger and am not sure why the 'elevator man' thought he had the right to impose this unwarranted behaviour onto me. I asked him more than once to get off me, to let go and I told him I was married and was not interested in him. He responded that he was also married and that he did not care that I was married. I was stuck! I could not move because he was a solid man and the pressure of his body weighed in on mine. I froze and was starting to feel nauseous.

It felt like the elevator was never going to stop. As the doors swept open there was Ricc and one of the managers of the company waiting in the hallway! Fu** what a relief, when I saw them! I was fu**ing furious and stepped out of the elevator screaming, telling the manager what his colleague had done to me.

This act of sexual harassment was uninvited and to this very day I will always remember that awful incident.

The 'elevator man' was a fu**ing bastard. I am glad I had a lucky escape.

EMOTIONAL DESTRUCTION

As individuals we cross paths with so many different people and every so often one extra special soul touches your mind and heart with all their being. Dalni has been that person for me since our very first encounter. I have always seen Dalni as a beautiful soul.

Each time Dalni has a salon visit her conversation is driven by a nervous energy, but at the same time it is also beautifully enchanting.

Ongoing drama wildly circles in Dalni's life. There are issues that involve drug addiction, physical destruction and violence, prison life and ongoing financial hardship.

Without question Dalni is a person who I have learnt many life lessons from. Listening to Dalni and her life journey is a story book in itself! Her own personal issues stem way back in her time. Although she had a good upbringing with her family, it wasn't until later in life that her real battles began.

When I first met Dalni there was always an energetic and fun element of cheekiness that stood out that I just loved about her. I wished for more happiness in her life but for the most part there definitely was a dark, dangerous and emotionally destructive pathway that stood before her. I felt so much empathy towards Dalni and wanted to support her in any way possible.

As the years went on and Dalni continued to share the story of her life with me, her embedded emotions continued to deepen. We named our salon catch up 'chat and release'. Dalni chatted and I allowed her that time to release whatever was on her mind. Two decades later what I do see is that slowly Dalni is crumbling. Her state of mind is weak, and I see a depth in her eyes that is heavy.

When Dalni burst into tears and said, "I will drink myself to death", I knew that she was on the brink of being dragged down further both emotionally and financially. Her fragile and weakened body made me feel exhausted for her.

The many experiences that Dalni has been through, and the emotional and mental scars deep down, are now showing as signs of exhaustion. When I listen to Dalni I can't help wanting to do more for her. I have come to realise that doing more won't ever be enough. It is about Dalni having the strength and courage to seek support so that she can move forward.

Knowing what I know makes it extremely difficult to accept that her daily life is the normal everyday life that she leads and has learnt to accept. In many ways Dalni is dependent on her husband Slay. He makes her work for every cent to fund her own way. In truth Slay has enough money to support his wife so that she does not have to tirelessly work.

Her battered and bony body is evidence of the hard work Dalni does on a daily basis.

I really love being in the presence of such a beautiful woman like Dalni but cannot help but feel sorry for her at the same time. Listening to her struggles and knowing that she continues to persist with day-to-day tasks and working commitments makes me annoyed. I am not annoyed at Dalni but at her husband! He does not support her financially and subjects her to a kind of abuse that unfortunately, many other girls and women I know also have to face.

On many occasions Dalni's husband would come into the salon with her. He would watch over us and would tell Dalni how much of her hair she could have cut. He would also decide what colour she was allowed to have!

At home and away from the salon, Dalni's husband would tell her what she could and could not wear on an outing. It was also common for Dalni to be out somewhere with a friend when her husband would unexpectedly show up without warning.

I totally understand why, after a day's work, Dalni comes home and drinks a bottle of wine to numb the heartache, her body aches, and the emotionally draining torment that she endures!

Dalni's journey to date is a constant reminder of what I see, hear and listen to from many other young girls and older woman who are victims to this type of behaviour. They are in relationships that are volatile, controlling and damaging.

To this very day, more than 25 years on, Dalni is still the battler, pushing through with a fragile body frame and still struggling financially as I had always known her situation to be. Yet she is still able to open her warm heart to you with her smile and that has never changed.

After Dalni visits the salon I cannot help but think of her and what she has told me in confidence! It makes me feel sad for her!

Hug me, I'm mentally tired.
@1positivewomen

FIGHT FOR FAIR

In most recent times, more than ever before, we are dealing with a very high percentage rate of mental health issues.

One thing I know for sure is that the feelings, emotions and connections we have with others can be a driving force for both positive and negative outcomes. When we are working on our relationships we often find ourselves being challenged in ways that perhaps we didn't think possible.

Unbosoming

There have been so many times that I witnessed a vulnerable person being taken advantage of by a bully, or a narcissist. To see people in dangerous situations being treated in such an unfair and unwarranted manner is debilitating, to say the least!

Will I call it out if I know someone is being unkind to another person? Fu** yes I will. Always! I am certainly not perfect myself however I do not like to see people be manipulated, 'screwed over' or made to feel sad and afraid at the expense of someone else's unacceptable behaviour!

Do I have the answers? No, but I do know that it is important to be socially aware enough to take notice if someone is in a compromising position that is affecting them in a negative manner or putting them in harm's way. Everyone's safety and wellbeing is important, no matter who you are!

If you voluntarily share something with me and are asking for my advice or help, I will always do my best to support you. I have seen first-hand that when someone is being mistreated by another person it can have such a profound impact on their state of mind which often leads to mental health issues such as anxiety and or depression, amongst other things. Overall, these issues can often lead to devastating outcomes.

I want to continue to make time for others and unless you tell me to fu** off or you don't need my help then know one thing for sure, I will never turn my back on you. I just won't!

I have had my own personal setbacks in life, but the people I really love I will always love. I may not like what you did or what I did or what we all did, but if you are important to me, I still love you! I still love me!

Violence, Harassment and Abuse

> "You have enemies? Good. That means you've stood up for something, sometime in your life."
> **Winston Churchill**

FINDING FREEDOM

Many years ago, on a busy Saturday morning in the salon, Blaire shared some very disturbing information about her personal life. I had no idea that Blaire was a victim of domestic violence. What I was told made me feel nauseous! I became infuriated and was so upset to see Blaire emotionally shattered!

As soon as I got home from work I immediately shared Blaire's story with my daughter. What I was told on that day really affected me! The reason I spoke to Brooke about this was to inform and educate her about the importance of being in a safe relationship. As her mother I wanted to create an awareness about domestic violence and I wanted Brooke to have a clear understanding that any form of abuse or domestic violence is unacceptable. Later that evening I also shared this story with my son. I went on to tell Corey that I would be absolutely enraged with him if I ever found out he inappropriately laid a hand on another woman. When Rachel, Corey's girlfriend, arrived we all sat together having an open discussion. I made it very clear to Brooke, Corey and Rach that if any of them ever felt unsafe or mistreated in their respective relationships, letting someone know immediately would be key to stamping out this cowardly and shitty behaviour!

As a society we must continue to educate young people, in fact all people, about the importance of treating others with kindness. Male or female, everyone deserves to be respected.

Say 'NO' to abuse and domestic violence. Together, let us all keep having conversations around this very important issue that needs so much awareness.

Over time my relationship with Blaire grew stronger. I wanted her to be free from this nightmare she had been living and made a promise that I would do my best to get her through this terrible ordeal.

Blaire continued to share many of her distributing memories with me and her stories kept coming to life, as though she was reliving the trauma she had experienced. It was as though her inbuilt secrets needed to be released as a way of starting to heal. The sadness and hurt on Blaire's face could be seen and the fragile sounds from her cries were just so devastating to witness.

Initially I was a sounding board to Blaire, a person who she learnt to trust. Our salon time together became more frequent, and the more I knew the more afraid I was for her. Blaire genuinely believed that with professional help things may have gotten better between her and her partner of more than 20 years. Initially, protecting her family secret was a priority. As time went on Blaire started to learn and understand that protecting herself, her three daughters and their overall health and wellbeing, was paramount in their recovery.

I never imagined that what Blaire told me would impact my life so much.

Blaire is not alone! I have had so many conversations with other women who have been victims of domestic violence and to this day some of them are still in toxic relationships. There are diverse explanations as to why these women choose to remain in these circumstances and each person has their own reason for staying.

It is really confronting when I hear these sad and frightening stories and to see these women break down in tears is just terrible! Most of them live in fear of what could happen next. The unknown is what catches them off guard. In any given moment a situation can unfold very quickly and the outcome can be extremely unpredictable and unsafe!

In Blaire's situation, the abusive behaviour continued to get worse as the years went on. Blaire started to believe it was her fault because she was always made to feel ashamed, and this pattern of behaviour escalated so much that she often lived in fear.

No one would have known any different if they ever saw Blaire out in the community, because she learnt to switch off in the presence of other people. When I would catch up with Blaire at the salon she would often appear emotionally intense and quite anxious, even a little scattered. Her confidence and self-esteem progressively started to shut down and her traumatic experiences translated into her dealing with ongoing anxiety, depression and mental health issues. She still suffers today.

I was keeping all of what I knew deep within me and would constantly speak to Blaire about confiding in family and friends so that we could support both her and her daughters.

As her daughters, Kingsly, Edith and Brydie got older, they were also being impacted by what they were witnessing. What was happening in their life was wrong on so many levels and clearly in this situation, Blaire, her partner and their daughters needed help.

Blaire kept telling me that no one would believe in her, that her partner would spin a tale that made her look like it was all her fault. I knew first-hand that he could undermine and bully Blaire.

I, amongst others, witnessed this behaviour on more than one occasion in the salon and out in the community.

Each time I would see Blaire at the salon I continued to listen to her stories. I kept trying to advise her that she needed to seek out support before it was too late. Blaire would instantly reply and remind me over and over not to tell anyone about what was discussed. If Slayton knew Blaire had told me everything, Blaire was afraid he would hurt her as punishment.

She continued to pretend that all was 'rosy', when it just wasn't!

So much of what Blaire told me made her relapse. All the trauma that she suppressed for so many years started to resurface. Her emotional state of mind was becoming very fragile. As Blaire continued to disclose all the awful memories that were consuming her about past experiences, I became more and more horrified. There are so many more stories I could share about the mistreatment that Blaire endured and it's really fu**ed up and sickening!

Everything about Blaire and what her and her three daughters were experiencing was of much concern to me. My mind and heart were aching for Blaire, Kingsly, Edith and Brydie. I was afraid for them and wanted them to feel safe again.

After some time, Blaire eventually confided in me that she was going to seek support for both her and her daughters. Although at one time Blaire and her partner spoke about counselling and guidance to help with their relationship, it never eventuated. He didn't want his abusive behaviour to become common knowledge to authorities or counsellors and so he continued to fly under the radar.

There was a time that Blaire had some unexpected health issues that resulted in her being in hospital. Thankfully her parents stepped in and saved their daughter from any ongoing physical abuse. I was so happy Blaire's parents supported her. Thank goodness for that!

Blaire and her three daughters are living on the outskirts of Victoria on a little hobby farm and unfortunately due to these current lockdowns that we are being faced with so often, I haven't been able to go on a road trip to visit them. We may not see one another but Blaire and I remain in contact and regularly chat on the phone. I can hear a more relaxed and happier tone in Blaires voice now. It gives me a sense of relief to know that Blaire is in a safer place with her three beautiful girls.

Behind closed doors the cruelty and abuse continue to escalate.

Evil is very deceptive, and the perpetrator can make things look good to the outside world.

Evil can be very clever.

It may appear that a perpetrator can be seen to the outside world in one way and live a secret existence in their enclosed environment in a completely different way.

HARASSMENT

I adored Lola. At only 23 years of age her working career came with a lot of responsibility. I thought wow, this young lady has an attitude that oozes drive and lots of ambition. I could always sense a level of maturity when Lola and I communicated. Her stories had a lot of substance and depth.

Lola had definitely witnessed many interesting scenarios in her management role. Being surrounded by wealthy, rich clients in her workplace came with no shortage of eye-opening surprises!
"Do you know how many celebrities come into the casino and gamble thousands of dollars away? We also see them crush up pills right in front of us, they then drop the powdery substance into their drinks and even snort it right up their nose as though no one is watching. And you should see the alcohol they drink; it is somewhat excessive and they just keep drinking! I witnessed one guy pee himself at the gambling table. He was so out of it that I am sure he didn't even realise what had happened! Some of the customers are pleasant and some are complete fu**ing arseholes. We call them arrogant pigs. One of the guys touched me on the arse and when I looked at him and told him what he just did to me was a form of sexual harassment he just smiled at me with a smug look on his face. Within a few minutes he touched me inappropriately again as though I was a no one!"

Lola was speaking a hundred miles an hour when discussing this incident with me. I wasn't surprised with what I was hearing. As we were talking Lola went on to inform me that many of the other women within her workplace had also been mistreated in this manner. The women often discussed their individual incidents between themselves but were afraid to come forward. As much as they wanted to inform their boss about their concerns, each of them just held back and said nothing! Lola and the other women had a fear of losing their jobs and were concerned that no one would believe them. When Lola disclosed to me that her boss suggested she perform a sexual favour for him, I wasn't shocked or surprised! Lola's boss also threatened her and implied that her position at work would no longer be available if she didn't comply with his provocative invitation.

At the casino, in this male-dominated space where Lola was employed, clearly some of these men in the high roller clubs that are loaded up with money, alcohol and or drugs, believe they are invincible and within their right to behave in such an unacceptable manner!

Despite all of that, Lola or any other woman should not be treated in a way that is insulting, rude or makes them feel uncomfortable. These types of behaviours are wrong and need to be called out!

Just like Lola there are so many women who have been victims to sexual harassment.

Sexual harassment is any unwanted or unwelcome sexual behaviour where a reasonable person would have anticipated the possibility that the person harassed would feel offended, humiliated or intimidated. It has nothing to do with mutual attraction or consensual behaviour.

Some examples of sexual harassment include unwelcome touching, suggestive jokes or comments, unwanted invitations to go on a date or requests for sex, intrusive questions about a person, body or private life, unnecessary familiarity, such as deliberately brushing up against a person, emailing pornography or rude jokes, among others.

If ever you are threatened or uncomfortable with any form of harassment I hope you can find your voice and the inner strength you need to let someone know how it made you feel. As a society we must continue to support one another with the injustices that individuals are being faced with each day.

Be that voice and make a difference in your life and the lives of others.

> "Our lives begin to end the day we become silent about things that matter."
> -Martin Luther King, Jr

NEVER TO RETURN

Father Leachman was the local priest and occasionally he would pop into the salon for a haircut.

As I got older I wasn't a regular church person and was only attending mass when I really wanted to. One day whilst cutting his hair he looked at me and asked, "Why don't I see you at church on Sunday mornings? I have not seen you attend for some time."

I replied, "Well I must say it's turned me off going to church knowing that so many Catholic priests have been committing acts of paedophilia. It goes against everything that I was bought up to believe. I thought priests were people who we could trust and that being in church was a safe place."

His face changed colour and his skin looked sweaty and clammy. I knew in that moment he was one of them! I felt disgusted looking at him. After that day Father Leachman never returned to the salon!

In time and just as I had suspected, the truth came out. Father Leachman was one of the many priests who has committed a crime of paedophilia and he was charged for his offences!

I get it. Yes everyone is human. We all make mistakes but for fu**'s sake, you are the priest!

It is no surprise that I started to doubt what I once knew to be the holy place of worship. It is very conflicting and contradictive to the church cohort when you have employed priests to lead the way and many of them have flown under the radar committing sins and getting away with it for so long. It is very clear that these men have needs, all sorts of needs.

My heart goes out to all the innocent victims who have been traumatised and scarred by these uninvited and unwarranted acts of behaviour.

'NO' to DOMESTIC VIOLENCE

Violent and abusive behaviours include mental, financial, physical, sexual, emotional and psychological abuse. Abusive behaviours don't discriminate and anyone of any age can be affected. We need to continue to find new strategies to help educate both younger and older people.

I have concerns about so many issues that people are facing in regard to abusive behaviours and domestic violence. It's a topic that needs immediate attention and a lot of discussion.

There is a growing awareness of the emotional harm and damage that people are living with as a result of being a victim to these abusive behaviours. It's got to stop!

No matter who you may be, we all deserve to be treated respectfully. Each person's wellbeing is important. As a society let's work together to ensure we have better outcomes for all. Your environment and your surroundings should be a safe place, no matter where you live.

As a society let us have a voice and advocate a message that any type of abuse is not acceptable. Period! Male or female, equally we must empower one another with these clear and very important messages.

Let us work together and find ways to provide current and up-to-date information about how we can prevent abusive behaviours, so that as a society, we can maintain safer and respectful relationships.

As a young person I witnessed behaviours from both men and women that are deemed to be unacceptable and unwarranted. As I got older I had no hesitation in having a voice to speak out. I will continue to be that voice when necessary and will always 'fight for fair' outcomes.

I have been criticised for my behaviour many times but have no regrets in helping others, especially if you have come to me with your concerns and have asked for my support.

Have you ever seen or heard people displaying acts of violence or communicating in a disrespectful manner towards another person? These are common concerns that have been brought to my attention from many different people.

Violence, Harassment and Abuse

I have so much more dialogue I could share but I think the following sums up a lot of the behaviours associated around domestic violence and abusive behaviours.

These are some of the things that you've told me over the years...

"My ex-wife is fu**en crazy! One time I ended up with stitches in my arm after she came at me with a knife."

"He's only hit me a few times. When he's good he's so great, I will be ok."

"Whenever my girlfriend drinks too much she becomes a person I don't recognise and there is no telling what might happen, like when she broke a glass bottle over my fu**ing head."

"My boyfriend grabbed my arm and then slapped me. Look at my bruises. It's okay though, he promised he wouldn't hurt me again."

"My partner has been beating me and pushing me around for more than 25 years. Whenever he hurts me he tells me it's my fault."

"I'm so scared, I don't know what mood he will come home in or what he may do to me. He hurts me all the time. Now he is starting to hurt the kids as well. What should I do? I'm really afraid."

"He will hurt me by grabbing my arm forcefully and I always end up with bruises. A day or two later when he sees my bruises, he demands I don't leave the house unless I cover them up."

"He threatens me all the time and says he will kill me if I tell anyone what's really going on."

"He dragged me out of the shower naked and then pushed me out the front door. I had to beg him to let me back inside."

"I get called a dumb c*nt all the time."

"He always tells me I am fu**ed in the head, that I have issues."

"My boyfriend pulled my hair and then threw me to the ground."

"I was on the floor and my dad kept kicking me uncontrollably."

Unbosoming

The list could just keep growing.

Anyone can experience domestic and family violence. It happens every day across all communities, ages, cultures and sexes.

We need to be open to these conversations with our children and others. The more we talk about it the more we can reach out to those who are at risk.

If you are the victim, let someone know.

We need to stamp out this cowardly, unjustifiable behaviour!
Look and listen to what's happening around you.
Do not let things go unnoticed.
If someone is feeling afraid and vulnerable, be that voice they need and support them to the best of your ability and do not be afraid to seek professional help.

> "It will be hard, but once you get out, you can live your life freely and get back the control that was taken away from you."
> **Domestic Violence Survivor**

ROTISSERIE

When Colson sat in the barber chair he couldn't wait to start chatting.
"My son Baxter and his mate Eli had a pig on a spit Saturday night."

I looked at him with confusion and had no idea what he was talking about. "What do you mean a 'pig on a spit'?" I inquired.

Colson looks at me laughing and says, "The fellas fu**ed a girl top to toe all night taking it in turns. One was fu**ing her while the other one was copping head."

That's exactly how he verbalised it to me!

I didn't think it was funny at all. I was disgusted that Colson just came out and said it the way he did. As a woman and mother of a daughter I started to feel insulted and uncomfortable. Baxter was 17 years old, Eli was 15, so I assumed that the girl involved may have been quite young.

Colson kept going on about it and even told me about the photos the boys showed him! I immediately thought, who else has seen or has been sent these images?

It turned into a debate rather than a chat and I decided to shut the conversation down very quickly. Over and out on this one Colson!! That was just way too much information and I could not wait for him to get the fu** out of the salon!

One in ten adolescents or teens have had embarrassing and damaging pictures taken of themselves without their permission, often using mobile phones. Sexting has legal consequences if the person involved is under 18 years old as it can be considered as child pornography.

REMEMBER, like any form of sexual behaviour you have the right to say 'NO' and to let that person know that you are serious!

As adults, we need to advocate respect and responsibility and look after the dignity of ourselves and others.

Unbosoming

VICTIM

Kelsy had to reach out to seek the support she required to ensure her health and wellbeing would improve.

For many, a journey of self-discovery can be very different depending on what you are going through or what you are seeking in your life. For Kelsy, her journey was an opportunity to heal and that was all her family and everyone else wanted for her!

Someone once told me that we create our own problems. Yes, I believe this to be true at times but for fu**'s sake, let us keep this shit real!

There are real victims out there who are deeply suffering. They did not create the problem they are dealing with; they fell victim to it!

There are many who have been victims to so many terrifying, destructive, volatile and heart-breaking situations and there are a lot of innocent people.

Nothing that happened to Kelsy was her fault, she was a victim. After many years, Kelsy learnt to become streetwise, guarded, protective and shielded. These became her barrier mechanisms, her armour. But all these shields weren't enough!

From what I know about Kelsy's past, her painful experiences have mentally and emotionally traumatised her. Kelsy's underlying fragile memories continue to haunt her. She had to seek professional help and I am so happy that she got the support she needed before it was too late.

I felt so helpless at times. I worried about the fragility I witnessed in Kelsy each time I saw her. I wanted Kelsy to smile again, to love herself and to know that she was important and worthy of being loved.

I do not see Kelsy often these days but when I hear her laugh, it's a laughter of joy, even if only for that moment.

When our past re-surfaces it can do one of two things – it can heal us, or it can destroy us. The relief is emotional and enormous when eventually you get to release the truth!!

We need to have more discussions and ongoing conversations about sexual harassment and abusive relationships. We must understand that any type of abusive behaviour is unacceptable. It is so important to build awareness, identify abusive behaviours, and take action to prevent harm to people in our communities, who may be family, friends, neighbours and/or co-workers.

# CHAPTER 7

My Lockdown, My Thoughts

CHANCE TO CHANGE FOR BETTER OR WORSE?

It is fair to say that my mind is spiralling out of control. Without wanting to get caught up in social media debates, I sit back and quietly absorb the chaos around me.

What I do know is that as a small business owner I have always maintained and addressed my responsibilities to the best of my ability. In doing so I have always looked after my employees with fairness and honesty. I have paid thousands of dollars throughout my working and business life towards personal, professional and tax obligations and over the three decades have provided my employees with an opportunity to build a career, whilst also offering a safe and happy workplace. The salon has been a livelihood for me and for others, and I am more than proud of myself for that.

Unbosoming

As a 51-year-old woman I feel blessed to have grown up in Australia. I will always remember our country as a place where we had freedom, real freedom. I felt liberated to do what I liked. I have never been bound to my home or forced to be locked up for the protection and safety of us all. Since the beginning of the pandemic, however, in my opinion I feel there have been inconsistencies and injustices. I am often left wondering, what the fu**!

Nevertheless, despite the ongoing rules that we are now living by, I can honestly say that I have had the best of 51 years in Australia. I have been free. No check-in, no codes, no vaccine passports, no identification checks.

As a business owner I have always valued each individual regardless of their sexual preferences, cultural background, religious beliefs or financial status. My door has always been open and welcoming to everyone, from all 'walks of life'. Now I am in turmoil. This pandemic has altered our lives and way of living and as a business owner I have to navigate my way in making decisions in order to move forward. Sometimes these decisions can go against what I truly value as I am torn between government directives and supporting those who have been the core of my business. I hope that in moving forward, continued support is given to small businesses. In the end I want to do the best for all without offending anyone, maintaining respect and continuing to uphold a professional service. Who knows what the future holds?

Our way of life and living has just started to have a major overhaul. There are social, technological and global changes that for me, and for many others, that can be fu**ing daunting!

My Lockdown, My Thoughts

MARCH 2020: LOCKDOWN 1.0

I have been procrastinating about how I would like to complete my book and decided to reflect on my thoughts that are a recollection of my life in 2020 and 2021.

Back-tracking to the beginning of 2020 and like many it started with a sense of uncertainty. It then escalated into more than I could have ever imagined!

As a business owner of a hairdressing salon in Melbourne, Australia, I was still deemed an essential worker! I was confused!

There were signs of panic and chaos starting to set in. I felt that our world as we once knew it would never be the same again. As the weeks and months passed by, we were continually faced with unpredictability and very much the unknown. There was doubt, hesitancy and an uncertainty about everything that was happening around us. As a wife, mother and a small business owner, like many others, I have felt helpless.

The first six months of 2020 became challenging, tiring and I was feeling deflated. The ongoing and sudden lockdowns fu**ed me up physically and emotionally. As a result of home isolation, just like many others, I was experiencing mental health issues and was feeling broken. Losing motivation drained me and I hated how it made me feel. Yet on the surface I continued to smile.

LOCKDOWN: 2.0 and 3.0

In the salon when we reopened between lockdowns I heard stories that just made me wonder how some people were coping. How were they making ends meet? So many had lost employment and the pressure of being in lockdown was affecting households in more ways than one.

Knowing some of my clients are victims of domestic violence made me feel afraid for them. How would they feel safe? How would they escape the torment, the abuse? Where would they go? I had messages from clients who were not able to get out of bed. On some days, I struggled with this myself. A common topic that always came to the forefront of a conversation was about young kids who would not come out of their bedrooms and were spending their days on social media. Then I had mums informing me that their kids were not fuelling their body with wholesome foods. As a result of little or no food consumption, isolation and ongoing lockdowns, they too were experiencing mental health issues. For some of these young children and teens this resulted in having to be admitted to either a hospital or an eating disorder clinic. One particular teenager I know overdosed on medication and was taken to hospital by ambulance. The parents of this young teenager were distraught!

Over time children and teenagers were becoming unmotivated, detached and were feeling alone and parents were struggling to find ways to help them. Parents are also struggling within themselves. The problems that are manifesting in our communities in relation to mental health issues have dramatically increased. I have heard of teenagers who are self-harming, and I know of people who have lost loved ones to suicide. I had a client call me distressed because her husband was physically abusing her in front of their children. Another client was sexually abused by her stepbrother, and it wasn't the first time! Some parents had no idea how their kids were feeling and often a lot of what was happening in their homes went unnoticed, unintentionally. We can all smile on the surface and seem as though we are in complete control of how we are feeling but underlyingly there have been pressures, heartache and emotional destruction, manifesting internally. It has been dangerous!

If I had an opportunity to disclose everything I know about what others had confided whilst in lockdown alone, I would be going on forever. It is another book in itself!

Listening to how others were feeling and what people were experiencing had made me feel anxious. I did not suffer with anxiety but now I was confronted with another hurdle. My stress levels were in overdrive and my mind was working overtime! It just felt like I was on a roller coaster going around and around, and then around again. Often, I felt dizzy, drained and discouraged!

Whether I was listening to a client, a friend or family member, everyone had a story to tell. There were many sufferings, and it was confronting to hear what was happening in people's lives. The information they were disclosing weighed heavy in my mind. I worried about them and myself.

Over time I also felt myself declining. This was further intensified when issues arose with my landlord. In 33 years I have never missed a payment; always loyal and responsible in maintaining my obligations. However, in July 2020, for the first time I needed to attend mediation. What a fu**ing low blow to the heart! My landlord must have been living on some other planet because when they put in a dispute against me, the outcome was as it should have been. I was not asking for anything more than what the government guidelines stipulated. Such a waste of time! As a result of mediation, I learnt that owing 'deferral' money for rental payment meant shit when I am playing catch up with no revenue. Like many other businesses that closed, the bills needed to be paid. If one more person tells me I will be fine because I am getting government grants, I say great, thank you! I need the help and so do all the thousands of businesses that are still closed.

Ironically the money has gone directly back to the government to pay my BAS statement or monthly salon rent plus outstanding deferrals, salon insurance, stock bills that are in arrears and on it goes. There have been people whose response to this is unempathetic as they are not experiencing this. To you, I say 'go fu** yourself'.

Aside from that I was getting ongoing emails that were 'doing my fu**ing head in'. This one read: "The owners have been in contact and advised as lockdown has all eased, they kindly wish to confirm the date in which you will be arranging the balance of the rental waived last month". It should have read 'deferred' but clearly, they made an error. If it was 'waived' then that meant I did not need to pay it, right? In reality the rental payment was not waived, it was deferred. Obviously, no help to me. I still had to pay it. I was not in the frame of mind to go to mediation again and the truth was that it was wasting my time and energy. I felt drained!

If I am being honest, what worried me the most is the aftermath of what has happened to so many people. We are just beginning to experience a mental health pandemic in Australia and all over the world. I really hope that there are lots and lots of people studying psychology because the demand for professional help, guidance and support outweighs the number of qualified mental health workers!

Whether you have been emotionally, financially or physically impacted on a personal or professional level, for many, it has become a reality!

LOCKDOWN 4.0

August 2nd, 2020, and Victoria is declared, State of Disaster.
It was during this extended period of lockdown that I began to feel like I had a virus in my soul.
My mind had become my enemy.
My train of thought took a shift in a direction that I was not quite used to.
I began to feel as though a painful darkness invaded and consumed me.
I did not like how it made me feel.
One thing I knew was that as humans we can be problem solvers. We look for reasons why things go wrong and them somehow endeavour to find the answers.
At times we get the outcomes we need to make everything okay again.
This problem, a world pandemic, Covid-19, clearly wasn't something for me to solve, nor anyone else.
Covid-19 is here to stay. Everything has changed, everything!

For better or worse I needed a turning point, for me. The chance to change how I was thinking and feeling was something that I needed to dedicate some attention towards. My mindset had to flow in a direction that gave me purpose. I began getting up at a reasonable time, walking Pablo, our family pet, every day, and discovering hobbies. I spent time in the garden, re-potted plants and began to make small progress with small tasks. I purchased a $2 bird tray and made it my morning mission to leave treats in hope that a bird would visit. Within a day more than one bird enjoyed my gift and although no one else in my home got excited about my visitors, I did. It was during this time that I also began to get all my notes and workbooks out of the cupboard that had been stored away for more than three decades. I had hundreds of snippets of paper with names and stories that I had heard over many years. Time allowed me to begin reading these stories. I felt like I was reliving each of those moments and listening to each conversation. Oh, my fu**ing goodness. I was freaking myself out and then just like that it happened. My writing began to flow.

> "Each person's life is like a mandala –
> a vast, limitless, circle.
> We stand in the centre of our own circle, and everything
> we see, hear and think forms the mandala of our life."
> **Pema Chodron**

LOCKDOWN 5.0

So much had happened between lockdown 4.0 and 5.0 and just when I thought I was getting on track, boom, here we go again! Announcement on Thursday 15th July 2021 puts Melbourne in shutdown mode! What the fu** is going on?

By Friday morning on the 16th July 2021, I opened up an email asking me to make payment to monies in deferral for my rent! I did not get out of bed until well after midday that Friday. This was weighing me down. I was broken! Those who know me would agree that I am a 'get up and go' person. I didn't allow myself to feel down often and am usually quite resilient, but fu** me, I was drowning in my thoughts. My mind and head felt like it was about to explode. I was consumed by the ongoing emails from the real estate agent and my landlord's intimidation. They made me feel negative, lethargic, inactive, sluggish and lifeless. "Give me a break for fu**s sake, we just went into lockdown again!"

On the 22nd July 2021 my next email arrived informing me that due to the nature of the rental market, and as a primary aspect of service to their investors, it was decided that an adjustment in my rent will take place in November.

Rental INCREASE!!! Is this really fu**ing happening? Are these requests normal? What a fu**ing nightmare!

My mental state of mind is exploding. Although I have time on my hands to sort this shit out, it is impacting my health and wellbeing as I am dealing with these ongoing setbacks. I feel so fu**ing exhausted!

Just as I am dealing with my own headfu**s and pressures, I have no doubt many business owners are also experiencing ongoing challenges. Hopefully their landlord is not as inconsiderate as mine!

LOCKDOWN 6.0

It's been an interesting week at the salon for many reasons and as we begin to settle back into some sort of routine and normality, boom we are fu**ing heading into lockdown again!

Suddenly we get an announcement on Thursday 5th August 2021 that at 8pm, not the standard 11.59pm, we are to lock up the salon and head home. In that moment and just like the past 20 months, life is a whirlwind! Spinning erratically!

It is now the morning of August 6th 2021, and I receive an email about the new rent relief that the government just announced. I proceed to pass the information onto the real estate agent and request they inform the landlord about the new government guidelines. I wonder what the outcome will be this time?

In recent lockdowns I was fu**ing shattered. So annoyed and concerned with everything that was going on. To share my thoughts has become therapy. It is a way for me to vent and release. Whether others support or agree with me is not my business, I just need to let go of the turmoil in my head!

Something else that really fu**ing pissed me off were some of the most disturbing behaviours I witnessed during salon opening hours. Some clients were rude when they were informed of the small price increase for our services. As a result of everything that is going on we were advised to make changes. As a business owner I am still playing catch up and will never make up for the losses we have encountered. We have to move forward as best we can. As much as I did not want to raise my prices, I had no choice! It is quite ironic, but the people who complained are the working minority. They are also the people who often complain the most about everything! Go figure! Deep down inside I am thinking what the fu** have you got to complain about?

In the handful of days when the salon was open, as usual, the stories and conversations continued to flow. The hot topic of conversation was the vaccine. The following stories are an example of people's experiences.

My Lockdown, My Thoughts

Bellsy got his vaccination and 20 minutes into his drive home he began to feel faint and weak. He then started to dry retch and in an unexpected moment Bellsy lost control of his car and hit a tree. Thankfully he is alive and well to share his story. Unfortunately, his car is a write-off!!

Lovely Dee just recovered from a four-week stint of feeling sick after her vaccination. The month that Dee wasn't well entailed her visiting her GP on seven occasions.

Karinne has a daughter in London who is aged in early 30s. Her vaccination led to a full burning body rash. Karinne's daughter is now unable to have her second vaccination. The hospital won't administer the jab due to what happened the first time and now she is afraid her daughter will not be able to come back to Australia without being fully vaccinated. Hopefully in time Karinne's daughter will be able to get all clear to come home.

We also had a visit from a lovely lady who works within our local community. We were gifted with a goody bag that has COVID treats including masks, sanitizer and information sheets amongst other things. We began to chat, and I asked the lady if she has visited our local shopping centre on her rounds. It was interesting to discover how some businesses had chosen to not follow protocol and for various reasons, it was okay.

Another thing that we experienced in lockdown 6.0 was a quarantine stint. One of my family members got notified on 8th August 2021 that they were at a Tier 1 site on the 4th of August 2021. They were informed that they could come out of quarantine on the 18th August midnight which is technically only ten days in quarantine. No one else in the home was asked to get tested. So, I am wondering about the four days of moving around before being notified to quarantine. I have no doubt that all the places they had been to in those four days, included lots of contact with others. Does that mean they were all at risk of perhaps being infected? Then two days before getting out of quarantine the same family member gets a phone call to be informed that they were at a Tier 1 site on the 4th August 2021. We were left dumbfounded and confused. When we called the appropriate organisation they confirmed that the family member was in the system twice and apologised for the mishap. The lovely lady we spoke to also confirmed that the system is flooded, the staff are overwhelmed and most employees are still being trained to work the system! I felt sorry for the lady we spoke to, she sounded exhausted!

Family member number 2 is notified on Sunday 15th Aug 2021 that they were at a tier one site on Monday 8th August 2021 and that quarantine is to finish seven days later. Yet again, for seven days prior to being notified, the family member visited the supermarket more than once, petrol station, partner's home and workplace. This is problematic!

Is the check-in system in place efficient and accurate, or does it have flaws? I have no doubt in my mind there are many flaws and inconsistencies with everything, and I mean everything!

Friday August 20th 2021, and in true form I get a reply from the landlord via the real estate agent that throws me off guard. I proceeded to get legal advice! Go figure!! Yet again I am only requesting what I am entitled to and do not understand why it's so important for my landlord to keep doing my fu**ing head in! I cannot believe it. Déjà vu!!!

My Lockdown, My Thoughts

UNEXPECTED DISASTER!

History is unpredictable just like every chapter of our lives and in August 2021 what happened to the citizens of Afghanistan is an indication that change is always happening. Where there was once hope, people are now facing the unknown. What is happening in Afghanistan puts a whole lot into perspective. It does not take away our problems in Australia, nor does it make our pain any less valid, but it reminds me that things could be much worse.

My heart is aching for the innocent men, women and children who are desperate to survive in such turbulent and destructive surroundings. My prayers of hope go out to all families who have been directly impacted whether they are in Afghanistan or around the world.

Will the people of Afghanistan ever feel safe? Will peace be restored? Is equality respected and recognised? How will these humans, desperate for a better life, find it?

In comparison, here in Melbourne the freedoms that have been stripped away from us seem insignificant. When you see the desperation and destruction in Afghanistan, you cannot imagine the suffering innocent people are experiencing. For better or worse there is a chance to change, but at what cost? The outcome after two decades of help and support has now diminished.

Although we may be worlds apart from Afghanistan, I believe it is also important to elaborate on the changes in our community of Melbourne that have impacted the lives of so many people in 2020-2021.

As part of my conversations, I am noticing more talk about mental health struggles. People have mentioned to me that they are struggling to get support and this makes me wonder whether there are enough resources around to support society's needs. I hope there are.

As humans we can sometimes go into survival mode so many times until we reach a point of needing help.

CONFLICTING CONVERSATIONS

I feel that there are some flaws and inconsistencies surrounding the decisions being made by the Australian Government. I believe that for a system to work well, the guidelines and road maps ahead should be consistent as a nation. As I continue to learn about everything that is happening around me, I have to wonder, what will the outcome be?

So where can I go and what can I do in Melbourne 2020-2021 wearing a face mask?

Well, that depends on which lockdown!

- Brothel (you can get your 'jiggy' on with a complete stranger, but cannot visit a friend or a loved one) What the fu**!
- Reject shop (My go to place for arts and crafts, not food, go figure? Wish Kmart was open!)
- Funeral
- Child care
- Wedding
- Osteopath
- Physiotherapist
- Supermarket
- Petrol station

My Lockdown, My Thoughts

- Care giving
- Alcohol store
- Cigarette shop
- Takeaway coffee shops
- Retail shopping plaza
- Outdoor playground
- Some doctors face-to-face
- Hospital treatments, some not all
- Building and construction keeps going
- No travel from home after 8pm or 9pm
- Outdoor exercise, two hours only, or sometimes three
- Teachers allowed in school to care for students
- Takeaway food outlets, including restaurants
- No travel more than 5km, sometimes 10km, sometimes 25km away from home
- If single, you can hook up online and go to meet a stranger for a date or company, WTF!

(I support meeting your friends and family as a bubble friend but a rendezvous with a stranger, seriously! People haven't seen family and friends for months or more than a year so I do not get that rule at all.)

Ok then, so what about where I cannot go or what I cannot do with a face mask in Melbourne 2020-2021?
Well again, that depends on which lockdown!

- Gyms
- Funeral
- Wedding
- Brothel
- Retail shopping plaza
- Place of worship
- Outdoor playground

- Bars and nightclubs
- Visit family and friends
- Hair and beauty salons
- Visit a loved one in hospital
- Dining in a restaurant or cafe
- Concerts and entertainments venues
- No pet grooming (which is a health requirement for some)
- 'Unexpectedly and suddenly' building and construction shuts down? Was this the last leg of the race to achieve the vaccine 80% quota? Once again left wondering?

Now I wonder. Although I support the Olympic Games and personally love AFL footy, I question why these have been allowed to continue after such strict measures have been put in place for all Victorians? I just want to clarify that my thoughts have nothing to do with what I love or what we love as a family. It is just very clear that the rules and guidelines are not fair for all. They differ and sometimes it is simply not right!

I am also left wondering – what happened to the entertainment industry during 2020-2021? Australian 'Arts and Culture' play such a significant role in our communities. It would have been great to sit at home (245 days and counting) to be given a choice. Sporting event, concert or a live show and performance. Just like sporting events with no crowds, I would have loved an evening of musical entertainment in the comfort of my own home.

I am so annoyed with the bullshit rules and privileges that clearly, are not the same for everyone! I am fu**ing pissed off that sport took precedence over what so many of us love and value because the fact is, not everyone loves sport!

Another issue that made me upset was knowing people could not get home! One of my clients in her 70s was stranded for more than three weeks in NSW. Not sure why a Covid test that reads negative and a home quarantine were not implemented in the planning system. Go figure?

Most of us have also missed out on celebrating Mother's Day, Father's Day, birthdays, Christmas and other special occasions with family and friends. Not everyone though!

There seems to be privileges and priority for some people. I just do not understand, nor sometimes agree!

My view is that our government and political system is in one league while many of us are in another. It is not an even playing field to see government members, politicians, AFL clubs, rugby teams, high-prolife celebrities and our Olympians, just to name a few, travel in and out of states, or overseas miraculously and conveniently!

For fu**'s sake there are so many people who haven't been able to visit a family member or friend in hospital or get home to say their last goodbyes to a loved one. So fu**ing inhumane and a load of bullshit! This makes me so infuriated!!!

To top it off, what are the $1000 gift cards and the 'million dollar vax' prize about?

Whilst there are many people queuing up at a food bank to be fed, there are also many under financial and emotional strain with the loss of a business, home or both. There are also 1000s upon 1000s of people who have lost employment due to vaccine mandates in the workplace, something I totally disagree with! On the flip side of desperation and distress, people are now being gifted with money to get a jab! What the fu** is going on?

SO FU**ED UP!!!

The year of 2020-2021 has left me wondering yet again about many things, but in particular I am fu**ing furious as to why we have apps tracing those who are in contact with a 'virus' but no apps tracing those paedophiles 'sex trafficking' our children? What a fu**ed up system!

WHAT HAPPENED TO OUR 2020-2021 HEROES?

Freedom of choice describes an individual's opportunity and autonomy to perform an action selected from at least two available options, unconstrained by external parties.

Our Australian medical professionals who were broadcasted as our 2020 'heroes' through the pandemic are now being discriminated and punished as part of the 'no jab, no job' campaign?

All the amazing doctors, nurses and paramedics, amongst others, have been at the forefront of working though the pandemic prior to mandated vaccinations. These same amazing, courageous and dedicated professionals have suddenly been criminalised and stood down. Humanity at its fu**ing worst. Our once 'heroes' who put their lives on the line are now jobless!

Recent government announcements indicated that Australia is importing 2000 medical professionals from around the world. These non-Australian citizens are coming into Australia to fill the gaps in our fu**ed up medical system whilst so many Australian citizens were not able to get home from overseas since the pandemic started! What a fu**ing disgrace to our country!

The divide in our communities is being instilled due to the dictatorship of our flawed government. Everything has changed!

My heart of hearts tells me that what is happening around us is an economic warfare. So many people are being faced with financial disparity and hardships that will continue to escalate. No jab, no job, no freedoms.

Vaccinated vs. unvaccinated, both can spread the virus, both can contract the virus, and both can be hospitalised from the virus. Both can still die from the virus, and both can remain completely healthy and have no issues at all! But yet, the two seem to be at war, like one choice outranks the other. It is time to stop judging others for their choices, it is creating way too much separation! I respect everyone's choice and believe we should have the right to decide. Clearly this has not been the case!

Open everything up and get the fu** on with it. Vaccinated and unvaccinated, people exist. We all exist!

The media is at the forefront of delivering our daily dose of news and it's so fu**ed up! I believe there are many important issues that are being overlooked and pushed aside. I have seen inhumanity and inconsistency at its worst. The mental wellbeing and negative state of mind of people is so disheartening. My belief is that the situation is getting worse.

ON A BRIGHTER NOTE: INSPIRATION, NEW POSSIBILITIES & TURNING 90!

With the negative experiences many have endured during lockdowns of 2020-2021, there have also been many stories of discovery and success. When things have been lost during this time, it has also been a time of finding.

Breathing fresh air and getting out in mother nature can have the most profound outcomes.

On my daily walks it was interesting looking around. I was inspired. Children of all ages had come up with creative ideas that made me smile. To see outdoor activities come to life was freshening, such as Spoonville, chalk writing rainbows, self-made bike jumps and nature strips turned into mini golf. These are just some of the fun activities that so many were enjoying.

During lockdown there were also many others who got creative with small business ideas.

It is amazing what can happen when you are forced to stop and slow down.

LITTLEREDHENGRAZING & HAPPY_ VANS (find me on Instagram)

I would like to congratulate Britt on her business venture. It's so special that your mum's collateral beauty will always be shared with family, friends and colleagues in our homes, workplaces and outdoor parks. Treating us all with 'Littleredhengrazing' boxes has kept Mum's legacy alive. Mumma Colleen would be so very proud of you!

I personally loved being in your presence as a giggling prep and am so glad that you crossed paths with Brooke. I have always loved your zest for life and am truly inspired by you. I wholeheartedly support your small business ideas and encourage others to follow.

Finally, I did get to meet with 'Henry' (the van). I was lucky enough to sleep with him. He was oh so cosy and listening to the rain drops on the tin roof was an added pleasure. I look forward to going on a road trip with him soon. I am waiting in anticipation to enjoy the luxury of happy_vans, once again!

Britt, you truly are something else!

Pluviophile;

A lover of rain; someone who finds joy and peace of mind during the rainy days.

LITTLE RED HEN GRAZING

Unbosoming

ZEAL

Rachel, you have grown to become an inspiring young woman who I love and adore.

As a small business owner and personal trainer, like many others in this industry you have endured full-blown setbacks with ongoing lockdowns. On the flip side, what I have witnessed from you has been astounding. Your new ideas, creativity, planning and preparation will certainly hold you in good stead moving forward.

I am excited to watch your progress beginning in 2022 as you embark on the next chapter of your life. With a new training studio on the way I have no doubt that a 'niche' personal space will attract many new clients.

Your turning point has transcended into a success both personally and professionally.

Your positivity and outlook on life is a credit to you!

Onwards and upwards!

Dreams really do come to life, and a once visualised idea, can unexpectedly come to the forefront of your newfound reality.

ZEAL.TRAINING (Find me on Instagram)

My Lockdown, My Thoughts

CELEBRATING LIFE AT 90!

A highlight of 2021 was the celebration of my Nonna Caterina's 90th birthday in March. It was truly special. The only gift Nonna hoped for was to have her family gathered together. The timing was perfect and Nonna was blessed with so many wonderful memories on such a significant milestone in her life.

PS: Thank you nonna for always having my back and never letting our little secrets be known! Well not until 30 years later! Hahaha

Love you Nonna X

Unbosoming

TEAM OF 2021

Maintaining a sense of stability and trying to ensure that my salon family are managing is important. I am continuing to do my best to provide them with ongoing communication, love and support.

I would like to thank and acknowledge my team Veronikah, Hai, Tiffany, Latifa and Kayla for being beautiful humans. You are all coping as best as possible during these troublesome and challenging setbacks, time and time again. In a year where there is still so much uncertainty, you have been the heart and soul of our salon. When I reached out and needed your commitment more than ever before, you didn't let me down. You are respectful, caring and kind, not only towards me but more importantly towards one another. Your ongoing loyalty and ability to endure everything that you are facing is a credit to you. I am lucky to be a part of your lives. Our workplace is a platform for you to showcase who you are and the kindness you express towards others certainly does not go unnoticed. Thank you for being YOU!

Finally, I am especially enjoying all our Messenger and Zoom gatherings over lockdown. Our weekend catch-up sessions have been great and to see all your beautiful faces is a bonus. Who says you can't have an awesome time over a screen? Games, fun, banter, booze, snacks and laughter! You guys rock!

What has been reinforced by this pandemic more than ever before and what I already knew is that teams and teamwork matter more than individual endeavour, at home, in our workplace and within the wider community.

My Lockdown, My Thoughts

THE NEXT CHAPTER

For me, going into survival mode and trying to stay positive has not been easy. What is happening inside my mind is real. What I am learning is helping me to progress. I seek support when I am feeling most vulnerable and I want to find a way to block out what is not working in my life. It is time to take a chance on myself and to make changes. Understanding how to best address my issues on a personal and professional level is something that needs attention.

Allowing myself the freedom to let go of everything that has been 'doing my fu**ing head in' has been an ongoing challenge. I have to find my mojo, my spark, and I know I will.

At times I may not have a get up and go attitude, and in truth, I am okay with that.

My daily mantra:

> I continue to allow my thoughts to be manifesting positivity, calmness and inner peace.
> I accept that I have many flaws and by making mistakes I will learn.
> Love and laughter is a great source of comfort and I am blessed with my nearest and dearest who share precious moments with me.
> **Cathy, 2021**

"Peace comes from within. Do not seek it without."
Buddha

To help my progress:

- I drink eight or more glasses of water daily
- I find solace and peace out in mother nature
- I love the aroma of burning candles and incense
- I listen to the sound and calmness of wind chimes
- I learn new recipes and enjoying cooking with pleasure
- I love the feeling I get when my bare feet touch the sand
- I walk for 20 minutes or more and make it a daily routine
- I cherish the love and hugs I get from my family and friends
- I most definitely love a sunset or sunrise and make time to watch it
- I often chat to the people who give out engaging and positive energy
- I love watching my garden grow and find time to appreciate what I created
- I savour and enjoy the food and wine on my kitchen table with family and friends
- I have enjoyed doing an eight-week 'ZEAL' personal fitness challenge. It was my first!
  I love how it made me feel both inside and out and want to maintain that feeling!

My new normality varied with each lockdown and so did my attitude. I still experience many fluctuating and fleeting emotions with each new day, but I am happy my writing was a constant source of support. Expressing myself has been my saviour!

About the Author

In 1975, my family relocated to Craigieburn. I was five years old and attended Craigieburn Primary School. I will always remember Miss Poulter, my all-time favourite teacher. To this day I still have a book that I was gifted from her. A special memory that has a place in my heart and my home.

Throughout my teenage years I always referred to myself as a country pumpkin. I would tell people that I lived out in the bush and being surrounded by paddocks and farmland confirmed exactly that!

In 1988, at the age of 18, I was unexpectedly offered to buy the business of which I was an employee. Before I knew it, I took ownership of a hairdressing salon in Craigieburn.

Lucky for me I always felt at home within the most colourful salon walls. I embraced the variety of what our industry had to offer and have never lost my passion for creativity. The salon was my safe space, and it is where I learnt to be a good observer and more importantly a good listener.

Unbosoming

What I enjoy the most is that every client service is different and so is the conversation. The art of 'listening' always made me curious and no two stories are the same. My learning experiences became more than I could have ever imagined.

As the days and months turned into years, Craigieburn evolved from a place to enjoy a 'country' living lifestyle into what it is at this moment in time – an overflowing community. As a result, the salon continued to thrive and grow into the successful business that it is today.

It is the year of 2021 and I keep reflecting about myself as that 18-year-old girl. How time flies! I am now 51 years of age (always 21 at heart) and after more than three decades of business ownership, I am ready for a 'SPIN AROUND'. I need a change in 'MY' life.

To honour a milestone of 33 years in business I decided to 'gift' someone the opportunity of a lifetime. My decision was made wholeheartedly, and I am very excited at the prospect of learning who the new salon owner will be. My hope is that 'Think Innovation Hair and Beauty', an already successful business, continues to flourish well into the future.

As for me and what I will be venturing onto, I guess time will tell. No expectations, no plans, just ready for a new beginning!

Appreciation and Gratitude

Despite my opinion about the inconsistencies I continue to witness, I am grateful to the government for their financial support. The business grants and individual payments that have helped to sustain keeping many of us going is not undervalued. For many though, it has still been extremely tough! What we are receiving is definitely a big help and I certainly appreciate it, but not everyone can make ends meet! I am older and have worked a long time and with the support of my husband and kids we are able to manage. That's not the same for everyone.

What I have learnt during the pandemic is crucial to moving forward. Trying to maintain an optimistic and positive attitude is more challenging than ever, yet it is important. I have faith in myself and others and look forward to happier days.

A big shout out to our community and surrounding communities. The salon, my second home from 1988-2021 would not be where it is today if it wasn't for our loyal clientele, past and present employees and the 'Indola' brand! You have all contributed and helped to keep our salon doors open. You made it possible for it to survive and thrive! Thank you for supporting my small family business in the heart of Craigieburn.

I also would like to acknowledge how privileged we were to have Jusdine, Angelique and Sue in our salon workplace for many years. You are without a doubt three of the most loved employees who I hold in high regard and are the most sought-after to date!

A massive shout out to my gorgeous nephew Julian for your expertise with giving 'Unbosoming' its initial social media platform. You are such a beautiful soul Julian and I would like to applaud you for having the courage to 'unbosom' a little of yourself. I will never forget the day we were sitting at the kitchen bench when you shared personal information with Zio, Frank and I. It really was a day to celebrate you!

On one last note, I don't give a fu** what anyone says, you will always be our best of the best, floorshow entertainment!

Brooke, Kayla, Lina, Luci and Rachel, you had the first set of eyes into my book. I thank you for taking the time to read and edit my stories. Your expertise, feedback and ideas were truly appreciated.

A very big thank you to ADNATE (Instagram). The artwork on the salon frontage has been a talking point in our community ever since it was beautifully created. I appreciate you allowing me to display and share your masterpiece as my book cover.

www.adnate.com.au

Photography: Mandy Sharman Photography and Kerry Kissel at LUSH Images. Always appreciate that you took time out to support our 'Hair Show' events and photoshoots. Thanks for everything!

Appreciation and Gratitude

Thank you Beccy, Maz and Lil for your professional advice, support and guidance. I could not have done it without you all.

To my sister Luci who constantly checked in on me and always touched base to see how I was holding up, I appreciate you more than you know. A big thank you to my sister Lina for your ongoing support and insightful conversations. Your guidance has been invaluable. Love you both dearly XX

Love you aunty Miriam. Thank you for all the beautiful messages. X

Justine, I am so grateful that you gave 'Unbosoming' the final edit on such short notice. I am now waiting in anticipation for some good times to be shared with you X

It is the small things in life that matter the most and I see it more and more each day!

Acknowledgements

I acknowledge the Traditional Custodians of the land on which we work and live, the Aboriginal and Torres Strait Islander people of the nation, and recognise their continuing connection to land, water and community. I pay respect to Elders of the past, present and future and acknowledge their spiritual connection to Country.

'Unbosoming' some of my thoughts has allowed me the opportunity to delve into my past. As I have reflected, there have been times I have been connected to people, and I am now at peace knowing that 'what once was' will not continue to be.

'Unbosoming' has also reminded me of the importance of being mindful of the present moment. Most importantly, in moving forward, I have come to realise what I want and do not want. I have found clarity.

Forever grateful to my parents. You took a risk and put up our family home as collateral so that I could get my first bank loan to buy a business. At the age of 18 it could have gone one of two ways. Even though I fu**ed up with some of the choices I have made in my life growing up, one thing remains and that is that I never lost sight of my responsibilities. I always knew that if I did not pay the loan, we would lose the family home, and you constantly reminded me of that! One of the best life lessons I have learnt!

Without the support of my husband Frank and our children Brooke and Corey, writing this book would have not been possible. Thank you for giving me the space I needed to allow my mental state of mind to be stimulated, engaged and proactive. It was therapy that kept me going in over 245 days of lockdown in Melbourne.

You all hold a special place in my heart and will always be the most important loves of my life.

Frank and Cathy

Acknowledgements

Cathy with Brooke and Corey

In and out of lockdown was made easier with my family and friends.

A special thank you to Frank, Brooke, Taylor, Corey, Rachel, Pablo, Kai, Dad, Mum, Laurie, Lina, Talia, Briana, Julian, Luci, David, Kayla, Blake, Lee, Michelle, Casey, Jesse, Indi, Daniela and Cristian, Nonna Caterina and family, Nonna Netta and family, Anna S, Annmarie, Aunty Angelina and family, Aunty Miriam, Aunty Ro and family, Brunella, Max and family, Bryce, Carl, Dafney, Silv and family, Dario and Dawid, Deborah, Steve and family, Dolores, Fordy, Hai, Tayla, Jason and family, Jenny@scoobsandswans, Jess, Jody, Josh and Kristen, Leesa and family, Lyndal and family, Marcus, Marie, Mary@AdeleLondon,

Unbosoming

Neil@chooch and Toni, Nick and Tee, Phil and Lena, Prue and Pino, Ricky@carpenter, Rose and Steffan, Samantha, Louie and family, Sandy, Ron and family, Sandy (Blondie), Tammy, Teresa and Veronikah.

2020-2021 was so much better because of YOU! Whether it was a conversation around the dinner table, a phone call, check-in via text message, FaceTime chat or exchanging words through music, it never went unnoticed! We may have laughed, cried, spent time together on a walk, managed to enjoy a holiday or had a fu**ing awesome time on an outing, to me it means more than you know.

Thank you for all the good times, the highs, lows and everything in between. I look forward to when we can all be together once again. I have missed our gatherings!

Extra special thank you to Tee for the best voice messages you have left me, the early morning texts and the FaceTime catch ups we have had. Love you X

Conclusion

Our new world and new way of living, whatever that may entail, is still unknown. I hope that as humans we take time to nourish ourselves and our sense of our worth. Somehow, we will get back to living our lives with a new and very different normality and whatever that may be for 'YOU' I truly wish you well. Be kind to one another and try to focus on being grateful for the good things in our lives.

In and out of lockdown 2020-2021 taught me to...
Make a plan, make it quick and make it happen!
If you were lucky, it may have been one of the best times of your life because 'time' is of the essence, and when we have the freedom to enjoy, we need to make every moment count!

Riccstar, you will sparkle within me forever.

Unbosoming
A Disclosure of Thoughts and Secrets
Cathy Vescio-Dibella

Cathy Vescio-Dibella is the author of 'Unbosoming', a book that integrates and shares her brand, legacy and personal memories, in the hope that it helps others to 'feel' something. 'Feelings' are the core of her stories. After 33 years in the hair and beauty industry, the stories told, shared and lived through have become a big part of her passion to help others undertaking a similar path.

In 2005 Cathy co-founded 'Body Culture' also known as 'Wheelz in Motion', a personal development health & wellbeing program that encourages individuals to build positive self-esteem, self-confidence and self-belief.

Cathy also participated in Shaping Futures – a global initiative program in the Philippines. This is a program that introduces disadvantaged young adults to the craft of hairdressing and provides them with the skills and support they need to escape hardship, unlock their potential and improve their chances in life.

A passionate and engaging speaker, Cathy supports young people to become more resilient and is a mentor to hair stylists and beauty therapists. Her desire is to better equip them with training tools to recognise, respond and refer clients, personal family and friends in need of help to the appropriate networks.

Cathy will leave you with easy-to-implement practical knowhow and inspire you to create the best version of yourself. Her motto is: 'Get up, dress up and show up'.

Cathy's signature presentations include:

Unlock YOUR Personal Brand
- Discover the Power of YOU
- How to be Noticed and Stand OUT from the Crowd
- Comparison is the ENEMY

It's a Love Thing
- How to Easily Put a Smile on Your Dial
- Your Vibe Attracts Your Tribe
- Seeking Perfection in an Imperfect World is a Recipe for Disaster

Mental Health for Hair & Beauty Professionals
- Recognising Unsafe Situations and Acting Fast
- Finding Support and a Safety Net
- Build Up Your Post-Pandemic Resurgence Powers

@ cathy@unbosoming.com   🌐 www.unbosoming.com

Reflections

Unbosoming

Reflections

www.ingramcontent.com/pod-product-compliance
Lightning Source LLC
Chambersburg PA
CBHW021141080526
44588CB00008B/155